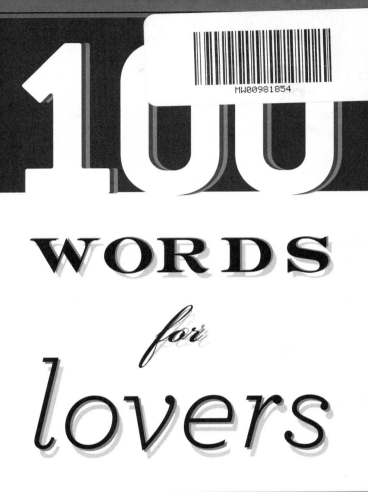

100

WORDS

for

lovers

THE 100 WORDS® *From the Editors of the*

AMERICAN HERITAGE®
DICTIONARIES

HOUGHTON MIFFLIN HARCOURT
Boston   New York

EDITORIAL STAFF OF THE
American Heritage® Dictionaries

MARGERY S. BERUBE, *Senior Vice President, Reference Publisher*
JOSEPH P. PICKETT, *Vice President, Executive Editor*
STEVEN R. KLEINEDLER, *Supervising Editor*
SUSAN I. SPITZ, *Senior Editor*
CATHERINE T. PRATT, *Editor*
LOUISE E. ROBBINS, *Editor*
PATRICK TAYLOR, *Editor*
PETER CHIPMAN, *Associate Editor*
NICHOLAS A. DURLACHER, *Associate Editor*
SOPHIE BLUM, *Administrative Assistance*

THE 100 WORDS ® is a registered trademark of
Houghton Mifflin Harcourt Publishing Company.

Visit our websites: www.ahdictionary.com
or www.hmhbooks.com

ISBN-13: 978-0-547-21257-9
ISBN-10: 0-547-21257-7

LIBRARY OF CONGRESS CATALOGING-IN-PUBLICATION DATA

100 words for lovers / from the editors of the American Heritage Dictionaries.
    p. cm. -- (100 words series)
  ISBN-13: 978-0-547-21257-9
  ISBN-10: 0-547-21257-7
  1. Vocabulary. 2. English language--Etymology. 3. Love--Quotations, maxims, etc. I. Title: One hundred words for lovers.
  PE1449.A146 2008
  422--dc22

2008039589

Text design by Anne Chalmers

MANUFACTURED IN THE UNITED STATES OF AMERICA

1 2 3 4 5 6 7 8 9 10 - EB- 15 14 13 12 11 10

Table of Contents

100 Words

for

Lovers

The 100 Words

Preface

It's a timeless problem, how to say what you feel, which words to choose, how to string them together. And the problem is never more troubling than when the subject is love.

100 Words for Lovers is intended to show how people have expressed their desire, their affection, their joy, their frustration, and their sadness when they are in love—talented and sensitive people coping with matters of the heart.

Specifically, the book places in evidence the words that creative writers and lovers in real life have used to convey passions, make themselves understood, describe the heart's complaint, and observe the ironies of romantic predicaments.

In this way the book is somewhat different from its predecessors in the 100 Words series, such as *100 Words to Make You Sound Great* and *100 Words to Make You Sound Smart*. These books showcase words that we all should know and put to good use in our efforts to be clear and convincing. They are primarily intended as vocabulary builders and reinforcers. They recommend words that we may have met before but don't have at our fingertips.

By contrast, most of the words in *100 Words for Lovers* are quite ordinary words, words like *desire*, *kiss*, and *passion*, that no one needs to explain to us. The point of this book is to celebrate these words as a way of coming to terms with the powerful movements of the heart and the fearsome dangers they entail.

To be sure, the book has some exotic and unfamiliar words, such as *callipygian*, *inamorata*, and *osculation*. And there are out-of-the-ordinary and somewhat formal words like *assignation*, *dalliance*, and *troth*. These words have their place too in the time-honored tradition of close encounters and communications.

To make its case, the book includes quotations from Renaissance and Jacobean poets as well as contemporary fiction writers, from recent film and television scripts as well as love letters from bygone eras. The English language may have changed, human culture may have changed, but the emotions remain the same.

And these emotions are what you will feel yourself as you read this book, the words and their quotations building like a wave from thought to thought, from page to page. To love is to live life fully, and this book is meant to help you make the most of every opportunity as you speak and write about love.

— **Joseph Pickett,**
Executive Editor

Guide to the Entries

ENTRY WORDS The 100 words in this book are listed alphabetically. Each boldface entry word is followed by its pronunciation (see page ix for a pronunciation key) and at least one part of speech. One or more definitions are given for each part of speech with the central and most commonly sought sense first.

QUOTATIONS Each definition is followed by quotations from poetry, fiction, movie scripts, personal letters, and other sources to show the word in context. The order of the quotations corresponds to the order of senses presented.

ETYMOLOGIES (WORD HISTORIES) Etymologies appear in square brackets following the quotations. An etymology traces the history of a word as far back in time as can be determined with reasonable certainty. The stage most closely preceding Modern English is given first, with each earlier stage following in sequence. A language name, linguistic form (in italics), and brief definition of the form are given for each stage of the derivation presented. For reasons of space, the etymologies sometimes omit certain stages in the derivation of words with long and complex histories, whenever this omission does not significantly detract from a broad understanding of the word's history. To avoid redundancy, a language, form, or definition is not repeated if it is identical to the corresponding item in the immediately preceding stage. The word *from* is used to indicate origin of any kind: by inheritance, borrowing, abbreviation, the addition of affixes, or any other linguistic process. When an etymology splits a compound word into parts, a colon comes after the compound word, and the parts (along with their histories in parentheses) follow in sequence linked by plus signs (+). Occasionally, a form will be given that is not actually preserved in written documents, but that scholars are confident did exist — such a form will be marked by an asterisk (*).

Pronunciation Guide

Pronunciations appear in parentheses after boldface entry words. If a word has more than one pronunciation, the first pronunciation is usually more common than the other, but often they are equally common. Pronunciations are shown after inflections and related words where necessary.

Stress is the relative degree of emphasis that a word's syllables are spoken with. An unmarked syllable has the weakest stress in the word. The strongest, or primary, stress is indicated with a bold mark (′). A lighter mark (′) indicates a secondary level of stress. The stress mark follows the syllable it applies to. Words of one syllable have no stress mark because there is no other stress level that the syllable can be compared to.

The key on page ix shows the pronunciation symbols used in this book. To the right of the symbols are words that show how the symbols are pronounced. The letters whose sound corresponds to the symbols are shown in boldface.

The symbol (ə) is called *schwa*. It represents a vowel with the weakest level of stress in a word. The schwa sound varies slightly according to the vowel it represents or the sounds around it:

a·bun·dant (ə-bŭn′dənt)   **mo·ment** (mō′mənt)
civ·il (sĭv′əl)   **grate·ful** (grāt′fəl)

PRONUNCIATION KEY

Symbol	Examples	Symbol	Examples
ă	pat	oi	noise
ā	pay	ŏŏ	took
âr	care	ŏŏr	lure
ä	father	ōō	boot
b	bib	ou	out
ch	church	p	pop
d	deed, milled	r	roar
ĕ	pet	s	sauce
ē	bee	sh	ship, dish
f	fife, phase, rough	t	tight, stopped
g	gag	th	thin
h	hat	th	this
hw	which	ŭ	cut
ĭ	pit	ûr	urge, term, firm, word, heard
ī	pie, by	v	valve
îr	deer, pier	w	with
j	judge	y	yes
k	kick, cat, pique	z	zebra, xylem
l	lid, needle	zh	vision, pleasure, garage
m	mum	ə	about, item, edible, gallop, circus
n	no, sudden	ər	butter
ng	thing		
ŏ	pot		
ō	toe		
ô	caught, paw		
ôr	core		

You never knew, or never will know the very big and devastating love I had for you. How I **adored** every hair of your beard. How I devoured you whilst you read to me at night.

— Dora Carrington, from a
letter to Lytton Strachey,
May 1921

adore (ə-dôr′)

verb

To regard someone with deep, often rapturous love.

> I cried last night Lytton . . . I cried to think of a savage cynical fate which had made it impossible for my love ever to be used by you. You never knew, or never will know the very big and devastating love I had for you. How I **adored** every hair of your beard. How I devoured you whilst you read to me at night. How I loved the smell of your face in your sponge. The thin and ivory skin on your hands, your voice, and your hat when I saw it coming along the top of the garden wall from my window. Say you will remember it. That it wasn't all lost. And that you'll forgive me for this outburst, and always be my friend.
>
> —Dora Carrington, from a letter to Lytton Strachey, May 1921

> JACK: As for your conduct towards Miss Cardew, I must say that your taking in a sweet, simple, innocent girl like that is quite inexcusable. To say nothing of the fact that she is my ward.
>
> ALGERNON: I can see no possible defence at all for your deceiving a brilliant, clever, thoroughly experienced young lady like Miss Fairfax. To say nothing of the fact that she is my cousin.
>
> JACK: I wanted to be engaged to Gwendolen, that is all. I love her.
>
> ALGERNON: Well, I simply wanted to be engaged to Cecily. I **adore** her.
>
> —Oscar Wilde, *The Importance of Being Earnest*, 1899

[From Middle English *adouren*, from Old French *adourer*, from Latin *adorāre*, to pray to : *ad-*, to + *orāre*, to pray.]

affair (ə-fâr′)

noun

A romantic and sexual relationship, sometimes one of brief duration, between two people who are not married to each other.

> The faint, floating sadness he always felt while locking up had to do with the time. In his experience, love **affairs** and marriages perished between seven and eight o'-clock, the hour of rain and no taxis. All over Paris couples must be parting forever, leaving like debris along the curbs the shreds of canceled restaurant dates, useless ballet tickets, hopeless explanations, and scraps of pride; and toward each of these disasters a taxi was pulling in, the only taxi for miles, the light on its roof already dimmed in anticipation to the twin dots that in Paris mean "occupied."
>
> —Mavis Gallant, "Speck's Idea," *Paris Stories,* 2002

[From Middle English *affaire*, enterprise, from Old French *afaire*, something to be done, from *a faire*, to do : *a*, to (from Latin *ad*) + *faire*, to do (from Latin *facere*).]

affection (ə-fĕk′shən)

noun

A tender feeling toward another; fondness.

> SETH [LORD]: What most wives fail to realize is that their husband's philandering has nothing whatever to do with them.
> TRACY [LORD]: Oh? Then what has it to do with?
> SETH: A reluctance to grow old, I think. I suppose the best

mainstay a man can have as he gets along in years is a daughter. The right kind of daughter. . . . I think a devoted young girl gives a man the illusion that youth is still his.

TRACY: Very important, I suppose.

SETH: Oh, very, very. Because without her, he might be inclined to go out in search of his youth. And that's just as important to him as it is to any woman. But with a girl of his own full of warmth for him, full of foolish, unquestioning, uncritical **affection** . . .

TRACY: None of which I've got—

SETH: None. You have a good mind, a pretty face, a disciplined body that does what you tell it to. You have everything it takes to make a lovely woman except the one essential—an understanding heart. And without that, you might just as well be made of bronze.

TRACY [*deeply hurt*]: That's an *awful* thing to say to anyone.

SETH: Yes, it is indeed.

—from the film *The Philadelphia Story,* 1940

HOLDEN: I love you. And not in a friendly way, although I think we're great friends. And not in a misplaced **affection,** puppy-dog way, although I'm sure that's what you'll call it. I love you. Very simple, very truly. You are the epitome of everything I have ever looked for in another human being. And I know that you think of me as just a friend, and crossing that line is the furthest thing from an option you would ever consider. But I had to say it. I can't take this anymore. I can't stand next to you without wanting to hold you.

—from the film *Chasing Amy,* 1997

[Middle English *affeccioun,* from Old French *affection,* from Latin *affectiō, affectiōn-,* from *affectus,* past participle of *afficere,* to affect, influence.]

alluring (ə-lŏŏr′ĭng)

adjective

Highly, often subtly attractive; enticing.

> Eddie Swanson, the motor-car agent who lived across the street from Babbitt, was giving a Sunday supper. His wife Louetta, young Louetta who loved jazz in music and in clothes and laughter, was at her wildest. She cried, "We'll have a real party!" as she received the guests. Babbitt had uneasily felt that to many men she might be **alluring**; now he admitted that to himself she was overwhelmingly alluring. Mrs. Babbitt had never quite approved of Louetta; Babbitt was glad that she was not here this evening.
>
> —Sinclair Lewis, *Babbitt,* 1922

> She was about nineteen, slender and supple, with a spoiled **alluring** mouth and quick gray eyes full of a radiant curiosity. Her feet, stockingless, and adorned rather than clad in blue-satin slippers which swung nonchalantly from her toes, were perched on the arm of a settee adjoining the one she occupied. And as she read she intermittently regaled herself by a faint application to her tongue of a half-lemon that she held in her hand. The other half, sucked dry, lay on the deck at her feet and rocked very gently to and fro at the almost imperceptible motion of the tide.
>
> —F. Scott Fitzgerald, "The Offshore Pirate," 1920

[From present participle of *allure*, from Middle English *aluren*, from Old French *alurer* : *a-*, to (from Latin *ad-*) + *loirre*, bait, of Germanic origin.]

---

amorous (ăm′ər-əs)

adjective

1. Relating to or indicative of love or sexual desire. **2.** Being in love; enamored.

> JULIET: Spread thy close curtain, love-performing night,
>   That runaway's eyes may wink, and Romeo
>   Leap to these arms untalk'd of and unseen!
>   Lovers can see to do their **amorous** rites
>   By their own beauties, or, if love be blind,
>   It best agrees with night.
>
> —William Shakespeare, *Romeo and Juliet,* around 1595

> Huge, spread-open Easter lilies were sticky with spilling anthers; insects chased each other madly through the sky, zip zip; and **amorous** butterflies, cucumber green, tumbled past the jeep windows into the deep marine valleys; the delicacy of love and courtliness apparent even between the lesser beasts.
>
> —Kiran Desai, *The Inheritance of Loss,* 2006

[From Middle English, from Old French *amoureus,* from Medieval Latin *amōrōsus,* from Latin *amor,* love, from *amāre,* to love.]

ardor (är′dər)

noun

Passionate sexual love.

> While the rustic feast was being prepared and dis-
> tributed among the sun gouts of the traditional pine
> glade, the wild girl and her lover slipped away for a few
> moments of ravenous **ardor** in a ferny ravine where a rill
> dipped from ledge to ledge between tall burnberry
> bushes. The day was hot and breathless. The smallest
> pine had its cicada.
>
> —Vladimir Nabokov, *Ada, or Ardor: A Family
> Chronicle*, 1969

[From Middle English *ardour*, from Old French, from Latin
ārdor, burning heat, ardor, from *ārdēre*, to burn.]

assignation (ăs′ĭg-nā′shən)

noun

An appointment for a meeting between lovers; a tryst.

> "Whither have you been rambling so early?" said Madame Cheron, as her niece entered the breakfast-room. "I don't approve of these solitary walks"; and Emily was surprised, when, having informed her aunt, that she had been no further than the gardens, she understood these to be included in the reproof. "I desire you will not walk there again at so early an hour unattended," said Madame Cheron; "my gardens are very extensive; and a young woman, who can make **assignations** by moonlight, at La Vallee, is not to be trusted to her own inclinations elsewhere."
>
> —Ann Radcliffe, *The Mysteries of Udolpho,* 1794

[From Middle English *assignacioun*, act of assigning, allotment (later influenced in meaning by French *assignation*, rendezvous), from Old French *assignacion*, from Latin *assignātiō*, *assignātiōn-*, from *assignāre*, to assign, allot: *ad-*, to + *signāre*, to mark (from *signum*, sign).]

attentions (ə-tĕn′shənz)

plural noun

Acts of courtesy, consideration, or gallantry, especially by a suitor.

> The songs took me right to the threshold of womanhood. I had outgrown my Littlest Angel bra and it had been a year since I'd officially become a woman. The combination of doo-run-runs and puberty was too strong to ignore. As soon as I entered Wagner Junior High I promptly fell in love with Mr. Dickerson, my seventh-grade science teacher and the first Negro teacher I ever had. Mr. Dickerson was boss! Mr. Dickerson was fiiiine. Beau fine. I memorized the leaves of every maple, oak, birch, gingko in Fairmount Park, but my love was unrequited. I did, however, get an A+ on my term paper, and inside the cover of the folder that contained my report card Mr. Dickerson wrote: "You are a terrific young lady. Keep up the excellent work." I got an A for the year. Still, my crush had been deep. I nursed my hurt for a whole year. By the time I was in eighth grade I had healed and was turning my **attentions** to a younger man.
>
> —Bebe Moore Campbell, *Sweet Summer: Growing Up With and Without My Dad,* 1989

[Plural of *attention*, from Middle English *attencioun*, attentiveness, from Latin *attentiō, attentiōn-*, from *attentus*, past participle of *attendere*, to heed : *ad-*, to + *tendere*, to stretch.]

beloved (bĭ-lŭv′ĭd)

noun

A dearly loved person.

> My **beloved** is white and ruddy, the chiefest among ten
> thousand.
> His head is as the most fine gold; his locks are bushy,
> and black as a raven:
> His eyes are as the eyes of doves by the rivers of wa-
> ters, washed with milk, and fitly set:
> His cheeks are as a bed of spices, as sweet flowers: his
> lips like lilies, dropping sweet smelling myrrh:
> His hands are as gold rings set with the beryl: his belly
> is as bright ivory overlaid with sapphires:
> His legs are as pillars of marble, set upon sockets of
> fine gold: his countenance is as Lebanon, excellent
> as the cedars:
> His mouth is most sweet: yea, he is altogether lovely.
> This is my **beloved**, and this is my friend, O daugh-
> ters of Jerusalem.
>
> —Song of Solomon 5: 10–16, *Bible,* King James
> Version, 1611

[Middle English *biloved*, past participle of *beloven*, to love :
bi-, around, thoroughly (from Old English *be-*; akin to the
preposition *by*) + *loven*, to love (from Old English *lufian*).]

10 besotted (bǐ-sŏt′ĭd)

adjective

1. Stupefied or confused by being attracted to or in love with someone. **2.** Characterized by foolishness or confusion caused by sexual attraction or love.

> MARY [BOLEYN]: Please don't be angry with me. You think I desired to go for this purpose?
>
> ANNE [BOLEYN]: All I know is that a man that didn't know who you were was with you in that room for half an hour and came out completely **besotted**! I don't know what you said . . . or did.
>
> MARY: Nothing, sister! Except sing your praises and talk about my husband.
>
> ANNE: Really? Well, you must show me how you did that sometime.
>
> —from the film *The Other Boleyn Girl,* 2008

> I was infatuated once with a foolish, **besotted** affection, that clung to him in spite of his unworthiness, but it is fairly gone now—wholly crushed and withered away; and he has none but himself and his vices to thank for it.
>
> —Anne Brontë, *The Tenant of Wildfell Hall,* 1848

[From past participle of *besot* : *be-*, thoroughly (from Middle English *bi-*, around, completely, from Old English *be-*; akin to the preposition *by*) + earlier English *sot*, to stupefy (from *sot*, fool, from Old French).]

bewitching (bĭ-wĭch′ĭng)

adjective

Emotionally captivating; entrancing.

> The way you let your hand rest in mine, my **bewitching** Sweetheart, fills me with happiness. It is the perfection of confiding love. Everything you do, the little unconscious instinctive things in particular, charms me and increases my sense of nearness to you, identification with you, till my heart is full to overflowing.
>
> —Woodrow Wilson, from a letter to Edith Bolling Galt, 1915

[From present participle of *bewitch*, from Middle English *bi-wicchen*, to cast a spell on : *bi-*, around, thoroughly (from Old English *be-*; akin to the preposition *by*) + *wicchen*, to cast a spell on (from Old English *wiccian*, from *wicce*, witch, or *wicca*, sorcerer).]

billet-doux (bĭl′ā-dōō′)

noun

A love letter.

> She left him as soon as their term at Guy's Hospital was over, so he could not locate her. She had plotted her departure for the end of term to avoid the harassment he was fully capable of; he was one of those men with time on his hands. *Cease and desist!* she had scrawled formally on his last little whining **billet-doux** before mailing it back to him.
>
> —Michael Ondaatje, *Anil's Ghost: A Novel,* 2000

> Mount Coffee-house, Tuesday, 3 o'clock. There is a strange mechanical effect produced in writing a **billet-doux** within a stone-cast of the lady who engrosses the heart and soul of an inamorato—for this cause (but mostly because I am to dine in this neighbourhood) have I, Tristram Shandy, come forth from my lodgings to a coffee-house the nearest I could find to my dear Lady ____ 's house, and have called for a sheet of gilt paper, to try the truth of this article of my creed.
>
> —Laurence Sterne, from a letter to Lady Percy (in its original spelling), April 1767

[French: *billet*, short note (from Old French *billette*, alteration of *bullette*, certificate, from *bulle*, seal, from Medieval Latin *bulla*, from Latin, boss, knob) + *doux*, sweet (from Latin *dulcis*).]

bliss (blĭs)

noun

Extreme happiness; ecstasy.

> EVE: . . . Confirmed then I resolve,
> Adam shall share with me in **bliss** or woe:
> So dear I love him, that with him all deaths
> I could endure, without him live no life.
>
> —John Milton, *Paradise Lost,* 1667

> And yet he trembled, sometimes into a kind of swoon, holding her in his arms. They would stand sometimes folded together in the barn, in silence. Then to her, as she felt his young, tense figure with her hands, the **bliss** was intolerable, intolerable the sense that she possessed him. For his body was so keen and wonderful, it was the only reality in her world. In her world, there was this one tense, vivid body of a man, and then many other shadowy men, all unreal. In him, she touched the centre of reality. And they were together, he and she, at the heart of the secret. How she clutched him to her, his body the central body of all life. Out of the rock of his form the very fountain of life flowed.
>
> —D. H. Lawrence, *The Rainbow,* 1928

[From Middle English *blisse*, from Old English *bliss*, from earlier *blīths*, from *blīthe*, joyful.]

blush (blŭsh)

verb

To become red in the face, especially from modesty, embarrassment, or shame; flush.

noun

A reddening of the face, especially from modesty, embarrassment, or shame.

> Small is the worth
> Of beauty from the light retired:
> Bid her come forth,
> Suffer herself to be desired,
> And not **blush** so to be admired.
>
> —Edmund Waller, "Go, Lovely Rose," 1645

> JULIET: Thou knowest the mask of night is on my face,
>   Else would a maiden **blush** bepaint my cheek
>   For that which thou hast heard me speak to-night.
>
> —William Shakespeare, *Romeo and Juliet,* around 1595

[Middle English *blushen*; akin to Old English *ablisian*, to blush, and Old English *blysa*, torch.]

15 **buss** (bŭs)

noun

A kiss.

verb

To kiss.

> She put her hands on his shoulders, getting a strong grip behind his neck, and pulled him down to where she could kiss him fair on the lips. A good long **buss**, like he never had from a woman in all his days.
>
> —Orson Scott Card, *Prentice Alvin,* 1989

> My lovers suffocate me,
> Crowding my lips, thick in the pores of my skin,
> Jostling me through streets and public halls, coming
>   naked to me at night,
> Crying by day Ahoy! from the rocks of the river, swinging
>   and chirping over my head,
> Calling my name from flower-beds, vines, tangled under-
>   brush,
> Lighting on every moment of my life,
> **Bussing** my body with soft balsamic busses,
> Noiselessly passing handfuls out of their hearts and
>   giving them to be mine.
>
> —Walt Whitman, "Song of Myself," 1855

[Possibly blend of obsolete *bass*, kiss (from Middle English *basse*, perhaps of onomatopoeic origin or akin to Latin *bā-sium*, kiss) and obsolete *cuss*, kiss (from Old English *coss*; akin to Old English *cyssen*, to kiss, and German *küssen*).]

16 callipygian (kăl′ə-pĭj′ē-ən)

adjective

Relating to or having buttocks that are considered beautifully proportioned.

> Without a glance in Mrs. Stone's direction, he gazed and preened in the glass, and finding it somewhat crowded by their two reflections, he murmured *Excuse me* and gave her a slight push to one side. Then he turned his back to the long mirror and, looking over his shoulder, he lifted the jacket over his hips so that they both, she and he, could admire the way that the flannel adhered to the classic **callipygian** shape of his firm young behind.
>
> —Tennessee Williams, *The Roman Spring of Mrs. Stone*, 1950

> "Don't go, Flossie," I said and stunned her. I'd known the Floss now and again, sumptuous knowledge, but not in a couple of years. It was past, my interest in professionals. I had a secretary, Frances. But now Flossie's breasts rose and fell beneath her little cotton transparency in a way that had been inviting all of us all night long, and when she had half turned to leave, when my words of invitation stopped her, I caught a vision of her **callipygian** subtleties, like the ongoing night, never really revealed to these eyes before.
>
> —William Kennedy, *Legs*, 1975

[From Greek *kallipugos* : *kalli-*, beautiful (from *kallos*, beauty) + *pugē*, buttocks.]

He lifted the jacket over his hips so that they both, she and he, could admire the way that the flannel adhered to the classic **callipygian** shape of his firm young behind.

—Tennessee Williams, *The Roman Spring of Mrs. Stone,* 1950

17 canoodle (kə-nōōd′l)

verb

To engage in caressing, petting, or lovemaking.

> SIR ALFRED: I took the further precaution of telling him the plot of "Cecilia," or "The Coachman's Daughter," a gaslight melodrama. . . . I filled him full of handsome coachmen, elderly earls, young wives, and the two little girls who looked exactly alike.
>
> EVE: You mean he actually swallowed that?
>
> SIR ALFRED: Like a wolf. Well, now you've got him, what're you gonna do with him?
>
> EVE: Finish what I started. I'm going to dine with him, dance with him, swim with him, laugh at his jokes, **canoodle** with him, and then one day about six weeks from now . . . [*A manservant enters with an enormous box of long-stemmed red roses from Mr. Charles Pike.*] It won't even take six weeks. One day, about two weeks from now, we'll be riding in the hills, past waterfalls and mountain greenery, up and down ravines and around through vine-covered trails, 'til we come to a spot where the scenery will be so gorgeous, it will rise up and smite me on the head like a hammer. And the sunset will be so beautiful I'll have to get off my horse to admire it, and as I stand there against the glory of Mother Nature, my horse will steal up behind me and nuzzle my hair, and so with Charles, the heel.
>
> —from the film *The Lady Eve*, 1941

To himself Edward was the same now as when they were first married.

"Of course after four months of married life you can't expect a man to be the same as on his honeymoon. One can't always be making love and **canoodling**. Everything in its proper time and season."

—W. Somerset Maugham, *Mrs. Craddock*, 1902

[Perhaps akin to English dialectal *canoodle*, donkey, fool, one who is foolish in love, or from colloquial German *knudeln*, to press, gather into a mass (as dough), cuddle with; akin to *Knödel*, dumpling.]

18 caress (kə-rĕs′)

noun

A gentle touch or gesture of fondness, tenderness, or love.

verb

To touch or stroke in an affectionate or loving manner.

> The hard look of anger faded from his face and it was as though a protection had been stripped from him and he were left bare, in the quivering, vulnerable nakedness of adoring love. His **caresses** were like the soothing of pain or terror, like the appeasements of anger, like delicate propitiations. His words were sometimes like whispered and fragmentary prayers to a god, sometimes words of whispered comfort to a sick child. Lucy was surprised, touched, almost put to shame by this passion of tenderness.
>
> —Aldous Huxley, *Point Counter Point,* 1928

We came to where the beach curved away out to the headland. I led her a little way into the trees, up a hill, and then sat down against a pine and made her curl against me. We kissed; tender-mouthed, though I felt too excited for tenderness. She let me undo the top button of her blouse and I caressed her throat, her shoulders. I ran my hand lower over a silky slip—her breast underneath,

---

almost naked. She caught my wrist then, holding my hand still, where it was. . . .

"Your body's so pretty. It's meant to be **caressed**."

She took my hand and kissed it; then let herself be cradled again.

She said, "Talk to me."

"What about?"

"About England. About Oxford, about anything."

So I talked; and she was touchingly like a child, lying there with her eyes closed, occasionally asking a question, sometimes saying little bits about herself, but mainly content to listen. The sky became dark. I kissed her once or twice, but it became a silent closeness, a lying touching, in which time soundlessly hurtled on.

—John Fowles, *The Magus*, 1966

[From French *caresse*, from Italian *carezza*, from *caro*, dear, from Latin *cārus*.]

19 charm (chärm)

noun

A particular quality that attracts or delights; a delightful characteristic.

verb

1. To attract or delight someone greatly. **2.** To cause someone to do something by strong personal attractiveness: *charmed the guard into admitting them without invitations.*

> What dress would best set off her **charms** and make her most irresistible to Ashley? Since eight o'clock she had been trying on and rejecting dresses, and now she stood dejected and irritable in lace pantalets, linen corset cover and three billowing lace and linen petticoats. Discarded garments lay about her on the floor, the bed, the chairs, in bright heaps of color and straying ribbons.
>
> —Margaret Mitchell, *Gone With the Wind,* 1936

> Dear Madam,
> — Not believe that I love you? You cannot pretend to be so incredulous. If you do not believe my tongue, consult my eyes, consult your own. You will find by yours that they have **charms**; by mine that I have a heart which feels them.
>
> —William Congreve, from a letter to Arabella Hunt, around 1700

ROWLANDS: . . . She **charms** you, I suppose, by her cool and assured air? By the impression she gives that everything in life amuses her—slightly? That is very engaging in so young a woman, isn't it? But you think that it is superficial, and that Vanessa can be transformed into a very different woman, and that you are the man to do it. You think that she will always be aloof and amused toward the world, but that toward you she will be the fulfillment of your heart's desire. Ice to the world and fire to you?

NICHOLAS: Shut up, Idris. You're going too far.

ROWLANDS: Don't talk like an officer in some imaginary 19th-century mess, Nicholas. I know Vanessa, and I know her father, too. She is something more than a match for you.

—Robertson Davies, *Fortune, My Foe*, 1949

[From Middle English *charme*, magic spell, from Old French, from Latin *carmen*, song, incantation.]

chaste (chāst)

adjective

1. Abstaining from all sexual intercourse; celibate.
2. Morally pure in thought or conduct; decent and modest.

> How have you passed this month? Who have you smiled with? All this may seem savage in me. You do not feel as I do—you do not know what it is to love—one day you may—your time is not come. . . . Do not write to me if you have done anything this month which it would have pained me to have seen. You may have altered—if you have not—if you still behave in dancing rooms and other societies as I have seen you—I do not want to live—if you have done so I wish this coming night may be my last. I cannot live without you, and not only you but ***chaste you; virtuous you***. The sun rises and sets, the day passes, and you follow the bent of your inclination to a certain extent— you have no conception of the quantity of miserable feeling that passes through me in a day.—Be serious! Love is not a plaything—and again do not write unless you can do it with a crystal con-science. I would sooner die for want of you than—
>
> > Yours for ever
> > J. Keats
>
> > —John Keats, from a letter to Fanny Brawne, July 5, 1820

[Middle English, from Old French, from Latin *castus*.]

clandestine (klăn-děs′tĭn)

adjective

Kept or done in secret, often in order to conceal an illicit or improper purpose.

> GRIFFIN [*pleading*]: Come on. What are you doing? Are you gonna tell me you've never had a good time with me over here? You *like* this. So do I. You like the **clandestine** nature of it. You *told* me that. You told me you liked going to nice hotel rooms. Come on.
>
> ASHLEY: I'd trade all that just to be able to walk down the street with you and hold your hand just once in public.
>
> —from the film *Sidewalks of New York*, 2001

> "Good God!" exclaimed Emily, "what an opinion must he form of me, since you, Madam, could express a suspicion of such ill conduct!"
>
> "It is of very little consequence what opinion he may form of you," replied her aunt, "for I have put an end to the affair; but I believe he will not form a worse opinion of me for my prudent conduct. I let him see that I was not to be trifled with, and that I had more delicacy than to permit any **clandestine** correspondence to be carried on in my house."
>
> —Ann Radcliffe, *The Mysteries of Udolpho*, 1974

[From Latin *clandestīnus*, probably blend of an unattested Latin *clam-de*, secretly (from *clam*, secretly + -*de*, emphatic or adversative particle as in *quamde*, how, as much as) and Latin *intestīnus*, internal.]

comely (kŭm′lē)

adjective

Attractive in a wholesome way.

> I stood a minute out of sight,
>   Stood silent for a minute
> To eye the pail, and creamy white
>   The frothing milk within it;
>
> To eye the **comely** milking maid
>   Herself so fresh and creamy:
> "Good day to you," at last I said;
>   She turned her head to see me:
> "Good day," she said, with lifted head;
>   Her eyes looked soft and dreamy . . .
>
> —Christina Rossetti, "A Farm Walk," 1866

[From Middle English *comli*, alteration (probably influenced by *bicomli*, seemly) of *cumli*, from Old English *cȳmlic*, lovely, delicate, from *cȳme*, beautiful.]

companionship (kəm-păn′yən-shĭp′)

noun

The relationship of companions; fellowship.

> For I have dreamed of her and seen
> Her red-brown tresses, ruddy sheen,
> Have known her sweetness, lip to lip,
> The joy of her **companionship**.
>
> —Paul Laurence Dunbar, "A Lost Dream," 1905

> Thus the two went side by side in a **companionship** that
> yet seemed an agitated communication, like that of two
> chords whose quick vibrations lie outside our hearing.
>
> —George Eliot, *Daniel Deronda*, 1876

[From Modern English *companion*, from Middle English *compaignyon*, from Old French *compaignon*, from Vulgar Latin *compāniō, **compāniōn-*, literally, one who shares bread with another : Latin *com-*, with + Latin *pānis*, bread.]

conjugal (kŏn'jə-gəl)

adjective

Of or relating to marriage or the relationship of spouses.

> Rose, after their separation, was long secluded within the dwelling of Mr. Toothaker, whom she married with the revengeful hope of breaking her false lover's heart. She went to her bridegroom's arms with bitterer tears, they say, than young girls ought to shed at the threshold of the bridal chamber. Yet, though her husband's head was getting gray, and his heart had been chilled with an autumnal frost, Rose soon began to love him, and wondered at her own **conjugal** affection.
>
> —Nathaniel Hawthorne, "Edward Fane's Rosebud," 1837

[From Latin *coniugālis*, from *coniūnx*, *coniug-*, spouse, from *coniungere*, to join, unite in marriage : *com-*, with + *iungere*, to yoke, to join; akin to Latin *iugum*, yoke, and English *yoke*.]

constant (kŏn′stənt)

adjective

Steadfast in purpose, loyalty, or affection; faithful.

> Let me see, what have I more to say?—nothing but the same dull story over and over again—that I love you to distraction, and that I would prefer you and beggary before any other man with a throne. I will call you Horatio— that was the name you gave yourself in that sweet poem—write to me then, my dear Horatio, and tell me that you are equally sincere and **constant**. . . . My hand shakes so at this moment I can scarce hold the pen. My father came into my room this moment, and I had just time to stuff the letter behind the glass.
>
> —Elizabeth Linley, from a letter to Richard Brinsley Sheridan, around 1772

[Middle English, from Old French, from Latin *cōnstāns*, *cōnstant-*, present participle of *cōnstāre*, to stand firm : *com-*, thoroughly + *stāre*, to stand; akin to English *stand*.]

26 **coy** (koi)

adjective

Flirtatiously shy or modest.

> A prior afternoon spent discreetly questioning proprietors of nearby shops had supplied the information she needed to find her way to Cole's door, for the man himself had been casually evasive. Indeed, the captain appeared to have a strong sense of self-preservation.
>
> Footsteps behind her made her hastily tuck away the key and chance a surreptitious glance askance. Her hopes were momentarily darkened as she recognized the tall, broad-shouldered form of Cole Latimer coming toward her. His brief, stiff smile as he swept off his hat was discouraging, but she plucked up her resolve and turned to face him with a **coy** laugh.
>
> "Why, Captain Latimer, would you believe that you're just the person I was hoping to see?"
>
> —Kathleen E. Woodiwiss, *Ashes in the Wind*, 1979

[Middle English *coi*, quiet, demure, reserved, from Old French *quei, coi*, quiet, still, from Vulgar Latin **quētus*, from Latin *quiētus*, past participle of *quiēscere*, to rest.]

His brief, stiff smile as he swept off his hat was discouraging, but she plucked up her resolve and turned to face him with a **coy** laugh.

"Why, Captain Latimer, would you believe that you're just the person I was hoping to see?"

—Kathleen E. Woodiwiss,
Ashes in the Wind, 1979

crush (krŭsh)

noun

A usually temporary infatuation or extravagant passion.

> DAVID: Sabrina, if I'd only known. Sabrina, Sabrina, where have you been all my life?
> SABRINA: Right over the garage.
> DAVID: Right over my car. Right up in that tree. What a fool I was.
> SABRINA: And what a **crush** I had on you.
>
> —from the film *Sabrina*, 1954

[From the noun *crush*, an act or instance of crushing, from Middle English *crushen*, to dash together, crash, crush, from Old French *croissir*, to gnash, crash, smash, of Germanic origin; akin to Gothic *kriustan*, to gnash.]

cute (kyo͞ot)

adjective

Delightfully pretty or attractive.

> It occurs to me in Bologna that there is no equivalent in English for the term *buon appetito*. This is a pity, and also very telling. It occurs to me, too, that the train stops of Italy are a tour through the names of the world's most famous foods and wines: next stop, *Parma* . . . next stop, *Bologna* . . . next stop, approaching *Montepulciano* . . . Inside the trains there is food, too, of course—little sandwiches and good hot chocolate. If it's raining outside, it's even nicer to snack and speed along. For one long train ride, I share a compartment with a good-looking young Italian guy who sleeps for hours through the rain as I eat my octopus salad. The guy wakes up shortly before we arrive in Venice, rubs his eyes, looks me over carefully from foot to head and pronounces under his breath: "*Carina*." Which means: **Cute**.

> —Elizabeth Gilbert, *Eat, Pray, Love*, 2006

[Short for *acute* in the meaning "clever, shrewd, discerning."]

dalliance (dăl′ē-əns)

noun

A usually brief romantic or sexual relationship.

> This was no time for softness, for sweet words, or promises he might not be able to fulfill. No time for even a friendly kiss, much less a **dalliance** with this woman who would fit so lushly in his arms.
>
> Dalliance? Where had that come from? He obviously wasn't thinking straight.
>
> —Jill Gregory, "Mirror, Mirror," 2003

> After that, even though she was dating a couple other guys, an assistant at the Michael Cohen Agency and a dean from the experimental college in western Mass., Thaddeus would turn up without notice, because things had to be flexible, and he would call from his car, coming down the West Side, and he would ask if now was a good time, never asking if someone was there but asking nonetheless, because he never expected that they were involved in anything but some amusing film-world **dalliance**.
>
> —Rick Moody, *The Diviners*, 2005

[From Middle English *daliaunce*, polite conversation, flirtation, sexual intercourse, from *dalien*, to converse politely, flirt, from Old French *dalier*, to flirt, perhaps from archaic and dialectal German *dahlen*, to flirt.]

desire (dĭ-zīr′)

noun

A strong feeling of wanting to have sexual relations with someone.

verb

To wish or long for; want.

> Suddenly, clearly, he could see her, the way he had been able to see her at twenty, not her physical self at twenty, because in every sense she was more beautiful to him now, but he felt that old sensation, the leaping of his heart, the reckless flush of **desire**. He would find her in the house, cutting fresh paper to line the shelves or lying across their bed on her stomach writing letters to their daughters who were attending university in Paris, and he was breathless. Had she always been like this, had he never known?
>
> —Ann Patchett, *Bel Canto*, 2001

> He resolved to wait until his accomplishments were so great that he no longer needed, as the male, to make the moves. He wanted to be **desired** and taken. He wanted to be all object, to have that power. He wanted to be that great.
>
> And so it happened that he was a virgin when he met Barbara and had been faithful to her ever since.
>
> —Jonathan Franzen, *The Twenty-Seventh City*, 2001

She was 55 and still a stunning woman when she looked him up this year. She admitted being very afraid of losing her looks, her lifelong trump card. She wanted to be **desired** again in the old manic way. Fitzgerald pulled back. The bitter irony of it: Suppose the divine woman of his fantasies suddenly surrendered to him, to his 65-year-old carcass, and it died on him?

"I don't want to be challenged on that level," he said forcefully. "At forty-five I was on top of the world. At sixty-five I am a very vulnerable creature!"

—Gail Sheehy, *New Passages*, 1995

[From Middle English *desiren*, from Old French *desirer*, from Latin *dēsīderāre*, to desire (perhaps originally meaning "to observe the lack of") : *dē-*, off, apart, away + *-sīderāre* in *cōnsīderāre*, to observe closely : *com-*, *cōn-*, thoroughly + *sīdus*, *sīder-*, star (from the Roman practice of making astrological predictions).]

dishabille (dĭs′ə-bēl′, dĭs′ə-bē′) also
deshabille (dĕs′ə-bēl′, dĕs′ə-bē′)

noun

The state of being partially or very casually dressed.

> She sank into the proffered chair, glaring at the discom-
> fited fat captain, and gave her name. The nice young offi-
> cer slipped on his overcoat and left the room and the
> others took themselves off to the far end of the table
> where they talked in low tones and pawed at the papers.
> She stretched her feet gratefully toward the fire, realiz-
> ing for the first time how cold they were and wishing she
> had thought to put a piece of cardboard over the hole in
> the sole of one slipper. After a time, voices murmured
> outside the door and she heard Rhett's laugh. The door
> opened, a cold draft swept the room and Rhett appeared,
> hatless, a long cape thrown carelessly across his shoul-
> ders. He was dirty and unshaven and without a cravat
> but somehow jaunty despite his **dishabille**, and his dark
> eyes were snapping joyfully at the sight of her.
>
> —Margaret Mitchell, *Gone With the Wind*, 1936

[From French *déshabillé*, undress, from past participle of
déshabiller, to undress : *des-*, prefix indicating the action of
undoing + *habiller*, to clothe, alteration (influenced by
French *habit*, clothing) of Old French *abiller*, to prepare,
strip a tree of its branches : *a-*, toward (from Latin *ad-*) +
bille, log.]

ecstasy (ĕk′stə-sē)

noun

Intense joy or delight.

> Since she decided to take this step, Manna had been possessed by a thrill that she had never experienced before. She began to have a faraway look in her eyes and smiled more to herself. At night she often felt as if she were in Lin's arms, her breasts swelling and her tongue licking her lips. She was amazed to find herself having changed into a rather voluptuous woman in a matter of a few days. She enjoyed sleeping without her pajamas on, although she was afraid that her roommates might see her naked legs if she kicked her quilt off in her sleep. The thought of spending an unforgettable day with Lin invigorated her limbs and filled her heart with **ecstasy**.
>
> —Ha Jin, *Waiting*, 1999

> Hot with skating and with love they would throw themselves down in some solitary reach, where the yellow osiers fringed the bank, and wrapped in a great fur cloak Orlando would take her in his arms, and know, for the first time, he murmured, the delights of love. Then, when the **ecstasy** was over and they lay lulled in a swoon on the ice, he would tell her of his other loves, and how, compared with her, they had been of wood, of sackcloth, and of cinders.
>
> —Virginia Woolf, *Orlando*, 1928

[From Middle English *extasie*, from Old French, from Late Latin *extasis*, derangement, terror, trance, mystical ecstasy, from Greek *ekstasis*, from *existanai*, to displace, derange : *ek-*, out of + *histanai*, to place.]

---

embrace (ĕm-brās′)

verb

To hold someone close with the arms as an expression of affection.

noun

An act of holding someone close with the arms as an expression of affection; a hug.

> It's no wonder Karen Blixen fell madly in love with Denys Finch Hatton in 1918. He was arrestingly handsome, intelligent, athletic and courageous. He was a war hero, a pilot and a lover of opera. The younger son of the 13th Earl of Winchilsea, . . . he was equally at ease in the African bush and on the country estate. . . . Who wouldn't want a swashbuckling lion slayer stopping in between safaris to recite poems and **embrace** her under the mosquito netting?

> —Florence Williams, "Under African Skies," *New York Times Book Review*, April 29, 2007

> He tossed aside the sheet and drew her into his arms. The strength of his body against her own suddenly seemed the most natural feeling in the world. Like the impossible and delirious new sensation of feeling his mouth on hers, kissing her deeply, searchingly. She felt herself responding to his **embrace** with an ardor she had never dreamed she possessed, her mouth demanding more and more. She couldn't kiss him deeply enough. His hands caressed her body, gently, then intimately. Yet her emotional excitement dominated all physical sensation.

> —Jacqueline Susann, *Valley of the Dolls*, 1966

When I was wont to meet her
In the silent woody places
By the home that gave me birth,
We stood tranced in long **embraces**
Mixed with kisses sweeter, sweeter
Than anything on earth.

—Alfred, Lord Tennyson, "Maud," 1855

[From Middle English *embracen*, from Old French *embracer* : *en-*, in (from Latin *in-*) + *brace*, the two arms (from Vulgar Latin **bracia*, from Latin *brācchia*, plural of *brācchium*, arm, from Greek *brakhīōn*, upper arm).]

enamor (ĭ-năm′ər)

verb

To inspire someone with love for another person; captivate.

> GINNY: I really love Rudy. And he is totally **enamored** of me. I mean, I've had men who've loved me before, but not for six months in a row.
>
> —from the film *Sixteen Candles*, 1984

> Unlike the intense, passionate Buonaparte, Hippolyte Charles was blithe and carefree, undemanding, with an easy social grace that lightened the mood of everyone around him. What was more, he was very dashing in his sky-blue hussar uniform with scarlet belt and red-leather Hungarian boots, black shako hat and fur-lined coat.
>
> Before long all the women were in love with Hippolyte, or so Josephine told Talleyrand. Therese Tallien, Fortunée Hamelin, even the cool Juliette Récamier were quite **enamored** of him. He was the beau ideal of the fashionable drawing rooms in May and June, his dark beauty a foil for the pallor of the women, who were just then following a fad for wearing blonde wigs. . . . With his fine features, olive skin, black hair and merry blue eyes he was quite irresistible.
>
> —Carolly Erickson, *Josephine: A Life of the Empress*, 1998

[From Middle English *enamouren*, from Old French *enamourer* : *en-*, in, into a certain state (from Latin *in-*) + *amour*, love (from Latin *amor*, from *amāre*, to love).]

enchant (ĕn-chănt′)

verb

To attract and delight; entrance.

> "If you really want to appeal to my better nature," replied Philip, "you'll do well not to stroke my cheek while you're doing it."
>
> She gave a little chuckle, but she did not stop.
>
> "It's very wrong of me, isn't it?" she said.
>
> Philip, surprised and a little amused, looked into her eyes, and as he looked he saw them soften and grow liquid, and there was an expression in them that **enchanted** him. His heart was suddenly stirred, and tears came to his eyes.
>
> "Norah, you're not fond of me, are you?" he asked, incredulously.
>
> "You clever boy, you ask such stupid questions."
>
> "Oh, my dear, it never struck me that you could be."
>
> He flung his arms around her and kissed her, while she, laughing, blushing, and crying, surrendered herself willingly to his embrace.
>
> —W. Somerset Maugham, *Of Human Bondage*, 1915

[From Middle English *enchanten*, to cast a spell on, beguile, from Old French *enchanter*, from Latin *incantāre*, to utter an incantation, cast a spell on : *in-*, in, against + *cantāre*, to sing, frequentative form of *canere*, to sing.]

Philip, surprised and a little amused, looked into her eyes, and as he looked he saw them soften and grow liquid, and there was an expression in them that **enchanted** him. His heart was suddenly stirred, and tears came to his eyes.

—W. Somerset Maugham, *Of Human Bondage*, 1915

36 **entrance** (ĕn-trăns′)

verb

To fill someone with delight, wonder, or love.

> Stolen to this paradise, and so **entranced**,
>   Porphyro gazed upon her empty dress,
>   And listen'd to her breathing, if it chanced
> To wake into a slumberous tenderness;
>   Which when he heard, that minute did he bless,
>   And breathed himself: then from the closet crept,
> Noiseless as fear in a wide wilderness
> And over the hush'd carpet, silent, stept,
> And 'tween the curtains peep'd, where, lo!—how fast she
>   slept.

> —John Keats, "The Eve of St. Agnes," 1820

[From *en-*, in, into (from French, from Latin *in-*) + *trance* (from Middle English, *terror*, trance, from Old French *transe*, passage, death agony, ecstasy, from *transir*, to pass, leave, die, from Latin *trānsīre*, to pass over, cross : *trāns*, across + *īre*, to go).]

37 **entreaty** (ĕn-trē′tē)

noun

An earnest request or petition; a plea.

> She had not noticed how he looked—only feeling his presence; but she turned deliberately and observed him. After all, he had been absent but a few months, and was not changed. His hair—the color of hers—waved back from his temples in the same way as before. His skin was not more burned than it had been at Grand Isle. She

found in his eyes, when he looked at her for one silent moment, the same tender caress, with an added warmth and **entreaty** which had not been there before—the same glance which had penetrated to the sleeping places of her soul and awakened them.

—Kate Chopin, *The Awakening*, 1899

[From Middle English *entrety*, from Middle English *entreten*, to deal with, plead with, from Anglo-Norman *entreter* : *en-*, in, prefix adding a notion of causation (from Latin *in-*) + *treter*, to deal with, treat (from Latin *tractāre*, drag violently, deal with, from *trahere*, to drag).]

38 **erotic** (ĭ-rŏt′ĭk)

adjective

Arousing sexual desire.

Camille was transformed through dance. Her somewhat squat, top-heavy body became a sexual dessert of curves and points. Her movements weren't the least bit exhibitionist. What was so **erotic** were the small but concentrated twists of her torso and hips. Every move and spin had a sexual confidence that didn't require a big flourish. It was the subtlety of her rhythmic rocking that was so exciting.

—Charles Busch, *Whores of Lost Atlantis*, 1993

[From Greek *erōtikos*, from *erōs*, *erōt-*, sexual love.]

39 escort

noun (ĕs′kôrt′)

The act of accompanying another person, especially as a protective guide.

verb (ĭ-skôrt′, ĕ-skôrt′, ĕs′kôrt′)

To accompany as an escort.

> I offer my arm in **escort** and lead her to the window. She doesn't release it when we get there. Her touch is nice, and we stand close together on this crystal springtime evening. The window is open slightly, and I feel a breeze as it fans my cheek. The moon has risen, and we watch for a long time as the evening sky unfolds.
>
> —Nicholas Sparks, *The Notebook*, 1996

> [*Katharine Clifton and Count Almásy dance together in the hotel ballroom.*]
>
> KATHARINE: Why did you follow me yesterday?
>
> ALMÁSY: I'm sorry; what?
>
> KATHARINE: After the market, you followed me to the hotel.
>
> ALMÁSY: I was concerned—a woman in that part of Cairo, a European woman, I felt obliged to.
>
> KATHARINE: You felt obliged to?
>
> ALMÁSY: As the wife of one of our party.
>
> KATHARINE CLIFTON [*sardonically*]: So why follow me? **Escort** me, by all means, but following me is predatory, isn't it?
>
> —from the film *The English Patient*, 1996

[From French *escorte*, from Italian *scorta*, from *scorgere*, to guide, from Vulgar Latin **excorrigere* : Latin *ex-*, out, forth + Latin *corrigere*, to set right (from *com-*, thoroughly + *regere*, to rule).]

flame (flām)

noun

Informal A person that one has an intense passion for.

> The frank honest face, to tell the truth, at this moment bore any expression but one of openness and honesty: it was, on the contrary, much perturbed and puzzled in look. Jos was surveying the queer little apartment in which he found his old **flame**.
>
> —William Makepeace Thackeray, *Vanity Fair*, 1848

> When Jimmie Trescott was told that his old **flame** was again to appear, he remained calm. In fact, time had so mended his youthful heart that it was a regular apple of oblivion and peace. Her image in his thought was as the track of a bird on deep snow—it was an impression, but it did not concern the depths.
>
> —Stephen Crane, "The Stove," 1900

[From Middle English, from Anglo-Norman *flaumbe*, variant of Old French *flambe*, from *flamble*, from Latin *flammula*, diminutive of *flamma*, flame.]

fling (flĭng)

noun

A brief sexual or romantic relationship.

verb

To throw (oneself) into a sexual relationship with abandon and energy.

> DR. DEREK SHEPHERD [*to Addison*]: Christmas makes you want to be with people you love. I'm not saying this to hurt you, or because I want to leave you, because I don't. Meredith wasn't a **fling**. She wasn't revenge. I fell in love with her. That doesn't go away because I decided to stay with you.
>
> —from the television show *Grey's Anatomy*, 2005

> ESTHER: Well, he's not very neighborly, I must say.
> ROSE: After all, he's only lived here three weeks. You can't expect him to **fling** himself at you.
> ESTHER: Well, that's true. Besides, meeting across the lawn for the first time would be so ordinary. I don't want to be just introduced to him. I want it to be something strange and wonderful—something I'll always remember.
>
> —from the film *Meet Me in St. Louis*, 1944

[From Middle English *flingen*, to rush (as to take up weapons), to strike (at something), to throw, of Scandinavian origin; akin to Old Norse *flengja*, to whip.]

flirt (flûrt)

verb

To act as if one is sexually attracted to another person, or to try to attract the sexual interest of another person, especially without being serious.

noun

A person who is given to flirting.

> She soon met *his* friends, the sorriest bunch of lecherous rakes imaginable. There wasn't one who didn't ogle her shamelessly, **flirt** with her, or banter with wicked insinuations. They were amusing. They were outrageous. And they managed to get her away from Anthony's side with one dance after another, until when she finally begged for a moment's respite, Anthony was no longer in sight.
>
> —Johanna Lindsey, *Tender Rebel*, 1988

> There would have been the making of an accomplished **flirt** in me, because my lucidity shows me each move of the game—but that, in the same instant, a reaction of contempt makes me sweep all the counters off the board and cry out: "Take them all—I don't want to win—I want to lose everything to you!"
>
> —Edith Wharton, from a letter to W. Morton Fullerton, June 8, 1908

[From Early Modern English *flirt*, to flick (something) away, fillip, perhaps of imitative origin.]

fluster (flŭs′tər)

verb

To make someone nervous or upset.

> Molly was **flustered**. She did not at all want him to go. No one of her admirers had ever been like this creature. The fringed leathern chaparreros, the cartridge belt, the flannel shirt, the knotted scarf at the neck, these things were now an old story to her. Since her arrival she had seen young men and old in plenty dressed thus. But worn by this man now standing by her door, they seemed to radiate romance. She did not want him to go—and she wished to win her battle. And now in her agitation she became suddenly severe, as she had done at Hoosic Junction. He should have a punishment to remember!
>
> "You call yourself a man, I suppose," she said.
>
> But he did not tremble in the least. Her fierceness filled him with delight, and the tender desire of ownership flooded through him.
>
> "A grown-up, responsible man," she repeated.
>
> "Yes, ma'am. I think so." He now sat down again.
>
> —Owen Wister, *The Virginian*, 1902

[From Middle English *flostring*, agitation, probably of Scandinavian origin; akin to Old Norse *flaustr*, hurry, bustle.]

gallant (găl′ənt)

adjective

1. Nobly or selflessly resolute. **2.** Courteously attentive, especially to women; chivalrous.

There was no use in trying to emancipate a wife who had not the dimmest notion that she was not free; and he had long since discovered that May's only use of the liberty she supposed herself to possess would be to lay it on the altar of her wifely adoration. Her innate dignity would always keep her from making the gift abjectly; and a day might even come (as it once had) when she would find strength to take it altogether back if she thought she were doing it for his own good. But with a conception of marriage so uncomplicated and incurious as hers such a crisis could be brought about only by something visibly outrageous in his own conduct; and the fineness of her feeling for him made that unthinkable. Whatever happened, he knew, she would always be loyal, **gallant** and unresentful; and that pledged him to the practice of the same virtues.

—Edith Wharton, *The Age of Innnocence*, 1920

"If the other seamen are as **gallant** as you, Billy, then I have no doubt the *Audacious* is manned by a crew of gentlemen." Her smile widened, bringing a glow to his cheeks and a buoyant grin to his lips.

—Kathleen E. Woodiwiss, *The Elusive Flame*, 1998

[From Middle English *galaunt*, from Old French *galant*, present participle of galer, to make merry, from Frankish Latin *walāre*, to live well, take it easy, from Frankish *wala*, well; akin to English *well*.]

heartthrob (härt′thrŏb′)

noun

1. A pulsation of the heart; a heartbeat. **2.** Someone who is the object of romantic interest.

> The glow which had risen to his face was reflected in hers, for at that moment it seemed as if it would be possible to love this cousin who was so willing to be led by her and so much needed some helpful influence to make a noble man of him. The thought came and went like a flash, but gave her a quick **heartthrob**, as if the old affection was trembling on the verge of some warmer sentiment, and left her with a sense of responsibility never felt before.
>
> —Louisa May Alcott, *Rose in Bloom*, 1876

> Misty and Lisa fought constantly over Roby, the assistant night manager. Roby was six foot seven and potbellied, with a high-pitched voice. An unlikely **heartthrob**, but he was the only male under fifty at Bunz. Even I carried a periodic torch for him, discreetly, of course.
>
> Lisa and Roby shared a trailer over the woods behind the Primate Center research facilities. That they lived together was little deterrent to Misty's overtures. Roby seemed irresistibly drawn to her boyish frame.
>
> —Sarah Thyre, *Dark at the Roots: A Memoir*, 2007

[From *heart* (from Middle English *hert*, from Old English *heorte*; akin to Greek *kardiā*, heart) + *throb* (from Middle English *throbben*, to throb, of onomatopoeic origin).]

---

idolize (īd′l-īz′)

verb

To regard with blind admiration or devotion.

> GREGORY: Candy, don't—don't leave. . . . I thought you were gonna stay.
> CANDICE: Well, we're done. is my shoe there?
> GREGORY: Well, Candy, I still have feelings for you.
> CANDICE: Greg, I dumped you for another man. How could you still have feelings for me? Besides, I'm still sort of with Paul.
> GREGORY: I thought that was over.
> CANDICE: Yeah, well, he was cheating on me. I guess I just wanted to feel better about myself before I see him to-morrow night.
> GREGORY: That's why you're here?
> CANDICE: Well, yeah. Look, you were always such a nice guy. But let's face it, we've nothing in common except sex, and the fact that you **idolize** me. I really do care for you. Really. I just can't wind up with you.
>
> —from the film *The Mirror Has Two Faces*, 1996

> NIGEL: What do you think you're doing sharing the details of your perverted sex life with a total stranger? It's just downright obscene!
> OSCAR: *Obscene*? Have you ever felt real, overpowering passion? Have you ever truly **idolized** a woman? Nothing can be obscene in such love. Everything that occurs between you becomes a sacrament, don't you see?
>
> —from the film *Bitter Moon*, 1992

[Formed in Modern English from *idol*, from Middle English, from Old French *idole*, from Late Latin *īdōlum*, from Greek *eidōlon*, phantom, idol, from *eidos*, form.]

illicit (ĭ-lĭs′ĭt)

adjective

Not sanctioned by custom or law; improper or unlawful.

> I walked slowly back to our room. The mist outside the windows was "soft" again. The only thing I could do was level with Nuala Anne about the castle. We would doubtless stay in the honeymoon suite, which was probably the master bedroom where Hugh Tudor and Augusta Downs consummated their **illicit** love.
>
> Great Fun.
>
> Maybe we could spend a lot of time on the golf course. If it didn't rain.

> —Andrew M. Greeley, *Irish Mist*, 1999

[From Latin *illicitus* : *in-*, not + *licitus*, lawful, past participle of *licēre*, to be permitted.]

inamorata (ĭn-ăm′ə-rä′tə)

noun

A woman with whom one is in love or has an intimate relationship.

> Tasso's loves were plentiful, a by-product no doubt of his restless moves from place to place; novelty of setting included the appeal of a fresh conquest. It would seem that a good number of these amours were literary rather than passionate. A few fine sonnets recording the new ardor sufficed to fulfill the desire. Such was the fashion of the day—languishing in verse, suffering lyric despair, and sharpening the quill to besiege the next **inamorata**.
>
> —Jacques Barzun, *From Dawn to Decadence*, 2000

[From Italian *innamorata*, feminine of *innamorato*, lover, sweetheart, from past participle of *innamorare*, to enamor : *in-*, into (from Latin) + *amore*, love (from Latin *amor*, from *amāre*, to love).]

infatuation (ĭ-făch′ōō-ā′shən)

noun

A foolish, unreasoning, or extravagant passion or attraction.

> As Edna walked along the street she was thinking of Robert. She was still under the spell of her **infatuation**. She had tried to forget him, realizing the inutility of remembering. But the thought of him was like an obsession, ever pressing itself upon her. It was not that she dwelt upon details of their acquaintance, or recalled in any special or peculiar way his personality; it was his being, his existence, which dominated her thought, fading sometimes as if it would melt into the mist of the forgotten, reviving again with an intensity which filled her with an incomprehensible longing.
>
> —Kate Chopin, *The Awakening*, 1899

[Formed in Modern English from the verb *infatuate*, from Latin *īnfatuāre*, *īnfatuāt-*, to make a fool of : *in-*, in, prefix adding a notion of causation + *fatuus*, foolish.]

inflame (ĭn-flām′) or enflame (ĕn-flām′)

verb

1. To arouse someone to passionate feeling or action.
2. To make a strong feeling more violent; intensify.

> His passions, **inflamed** by disappointment, and strengthened by repulse, now defied the power of obstacle; and those considerations which would have operated with a more delicate mind to overcome its original inclination, served only to increase the violence of his.
>
> —Ann Radcliffe, *A Sicilian Romance*, 1790

> He awoke heated and unrefreshed. During his sleep, his **inflamed** imagination had presented him with none but the most voluptuous objects. Matilda stood before him in his dreams, and his eyes again dwelt upon her naked breast; she repeated her protestations of eternal love, threw her arms round his neck, and loaded him with kisses: he returned them; he clasped her passionately to his bosom, and—the vision was dissolved.
>
> —Matthew Gregory Lewis, *The Monk*, 1796

[From Middle English *enflaumen*, from Old French *enflammer*, from Latin *īnflammāre* : *in-*, in, intensive prefix + *flammāre*, to set on fire (from *flamma*, flame).]

intimate (ĭn′tə-mĭt)

adjective

Characterized by close personal acquaintance or familiarity.

> Again at eight o'clock, when the dark lanes of the Forties were lined five deep with throbbing taxicabs, bound for the theatre district, I felt a sinking in my heart. Forms leaned together in the taxis as they waited, and voices sang, and there was laughter from unheard jokes, and lighted cigarettes made unintelligible circles inside. Imagining that I, too, was hurrying towards gaiety and sharing their **intimate** excitement, I wished them well.
>
> —F. Scott Fitzgerald, *The Great Gatsby*, 1925

> I should have liked to have dined with you today, after finishing your essay—that my eyes, and lips, I do not exactly mean my voice, might have told you that they had raised you in my esteem. What a cold word! I would say love, if you will promise not to dispute about its propriety, when I want to express an increasing affection, founded on a more **intimate** acquaintance with your heart and understanding. . . . You know not how much tenderness for you may escape in a voluptuous sigh, should the air, as is often the case, give a pleasurable movement to the sensations, that have been clustering round my heart, as I read this morning—reminding myself, every now and then, that the writer loved me.
>
> —Mary Wollstonecraft, from a letter to William Godwin, October 4, 1796

[From Latin *intimātus*, past participle of *intimāre*, to make familiar with, from *intimus*, innermost; akin to Latin *inter*, between, surrounded by, and English *in*.]

---

intimate   58

Again at eight o'clock, when the dark lanes of the Forties were lined five deep with throbbing taxicabs, bound for the theatre district, I felt a sinking in my heart. Forms leaned together in the taxis as they waited, and voices sang, and there was laughter from unheard jokes, and lighted cigarettes made unintelligible circles inside. Imagining that I, too, was hurrying towards gaiety and sharing their **intimate** excitement, I wished them well.

—F. Scott Fitzgerald, *The Great Gatsby*, 1925

intoxicating (ĭn-tŏk′sĭ-kāt′ĭng)

adjective

Stupefying or exciting, as if by having consumed too much alcohol or a narcotic.

> She stood up from the table, swaying slightly because she was not used to drinking so much. "I absolutely have to go," she said, feeling dizzy and light-headed. "Please say good night to everyone for me."
>
> He stood also. He was much taller than she, and he had extremely broad shoulders. He smelled of some masculine scent that she found quite **intoxicating**.
>
> "I will escort you home and come back," he said.
>
> —Jackie Collins, *Dangerous Kiss*, 1999

[From present participle of *intoxicate*, from Middle English, to poison, from Medieval Latin *intoxicāre*, *intoxicāt-* : Latin *in-*, in + Late Latin *toxicāre*, to smear with poison (from Latin *toxicum*, poison, from Greek *toxikon*, poison for arrows, poison, from neuter of *toxikos*, of a bow, from *toxon*, bow, from Old Iranian *taxša-, arrow).]

jealousy (jĕl′ə-sē)

noun

A state of being fearful of losing one's lover to someone else or of being suspicious that a lover is being unfaithful.

> It could not go on without some sort of convulsion, and that Christmas was a time of recriminations. Angela's infatuation was growing, and she did not always hide this from Stephen. Letters would arrive in Roger's handwriting, and Stephen, half crazy with **jealousy** by now, would demand to see them.
>
> —Radclyffe Hall, *The Well of Loneliness*, 1928

> But she smiled, he saw, only out of politeness, and he felt a flash of **jealousy** as do friends when they lose another to love, especially those who have understood that friendship is enough, steadier, healthier, easier on the heart. Something that always added and never took away.
>
> —Kiran Desai, *The Inheritance of Loss*, 2006

[From Middle English *gelosie*, from Old French, from *gelos*, zealous, jealous, from Vulgar Latin **zēlōsus*, from Late Latin *zēlus*, zeal, from Greek *zēlos*.]

54 **jilt** (jĭlt)

verb

To deceive or abandon (a lover) suddenly or callously.

> "So, Lizzy," said he one day, "your sister is crossed in love I find. I congratulate her. Next to being married, a girl likes to be crossed in love a little now and then. It is something to think of, and gives her a sort of distinction among her companions. When is your turn to come? You will hardly bear to be long outdone by Jane. Now is your time. Here are officers enough at Meryton to disappoint all the young ladies in the country. Let Wickham be your man. He is a pleasant fellow, and would **jilt** you creditably."
>
> —Jane Austen, *Pride and Prejudice*, 1813

[Possibly from obsolete *jilt*, harlot, alteration of *gillot*, diminutive of *gille*, woman, girl, from Middle English, from *Gille*, a woman's name.]

55 **kiss** (kĭs)

verb

To touch another person with the lips as an expression of affection, greeting, respect, or amorousness.

noun

A touch of one person by another with the lips.

> His heart beat faster and faster as Daisy's white face came up to his own. He knew that when he **kissed** this girl, and forever wed his unutterable visions to her per-

ishable breath, his mind would never romp again like the mind of God. So he waited, listening for a moment longer to the tuning-fork that had been struck upon a star. Then he kissed her. At his lips' touch she blossomed for him like a flower and the incarnation was complete.

—F. Scott Fitzgerald, *The Great Gatsby*, 1925

He was so close to her then that they owned every molecule of air in the tiny room and the air grew heavy with their desire and worked to move them together. It was with the smallest step forward that his face was in her hair and then her arms were around his back and they were holding each other. It seemed so simple to get to this place, such a magnificent relief, that he couldn't imagine why he had not been holding her every minute since they first met. . . . Carmen leaned forward and **kissed** him. There was no time for kissing but she wanted him to know that in the future there would be. A kiss in so much loneliness was like a hand pulling you up out of the water, scooping you up from a place of drowning and into the reckless abundance of air. A kiss, another kiss. "Go," she whispered.

—Ann Patchett, *Bel Canto*, 2001

[From Middle English *kissen*, from Old English *cyssan*; akin to German *küssen* and Norwegian and Swedish *kyssa*.]

languor (lăng′gər, lăng′ər)

noun

1. Lack of physical or mental energy; listlessness. **2.** A dreamy, lazy mood or quality.

> To my eyes also love and sympathy brought the tears; but in a little while the fond, comforting words I spoke and my caresses recalled her from that sad past to the present; then, lying back as at first, her head resting on my folded cloak, her body partly supported by my encircling arm and partly by the rock we were leaning against, her half-closed eyes turned to mine expressed a tender assured happiness—the chastened gladness of sunshine after rain; a soft delicious **languor** that was partly passionate with the passion etherealized.
>
> —W. H. Hudson, *Green Mansions*, 1904

[From Middle English *langour*, from Old French *langor*, *langueur*, from Latin *languor*, from *languēre*, to be languid; akin to English *slack*.]

liaison (lē′ā-zŏn′, lē-ā′zŏn′)

noun

A sexual relationship, especially an adulterous one; an affair.

> When the rumour of his **liaison** with Miss Dunstable reached her ears, when she heard of Miss Dunstable's fortune, she had wept, wept outright, in her chamber—wept, as she said to herself, to think that he should be so mercenary; but she had wept, as she should have said to herself, at finding that he was so faithless. Then, when

she knew at last that this rumour was false, when she found that she was banished from Greshamsbury for his sake, when she was forced to retreat with her friend Patience, how could she but love him, in that he was not mercenary? How could she not love him in that he was so faithful?

—Anthony Trollope, *Doctor Thorne*, 1858

JANETTE [North]: Gee, I can hardly wait to meet him!

COLLEEN [North]: Mmm, me too!

HELEN [North]: Uh, let's not overwhelm him with family—not the first date, huh?

JEAN [North]: You mean he doesn't know about us?

HELEN: Well of course he does, darling!

JEAN: All of us?

COLLEEN: Oh mother, that's so romantic! You lied to him!

HELEN: I did not lie to him! I just didn't have the nerve to tell him the whole truth!

COLLEEN: Mmm, I understand. No man wants a **liaison** with a woman with eight children!

JANETTE: What's a liaison?

COLLEEN: An affair.

JANETTE: That's what I thought.

JEAN: Me too.

HELEN: I am not having an affair! And I'm not having a liaison. I'm merely going to dinner. And as soon as I tell him about all of you, he'll bring me home in plenty of time for dessert.

—from the film *Yours, Mine and Ours*, 1968

[From French, connection, intimacy, from Old French, from Latin *ligātiō*, *ligātiōn-*, a binding, from *ligātus*, past participle of *ligāre*, to bind.]

love (lŭv)

noun

A feeling of intense desire, attraction, and concern toward someone; the emotion of sex and romance.

verb

To feel love toward someone; have an intense emotional attachment to someone.

> But one couldn't believe that reading *Jane Eyre* was wrong. And if it were, if at fourteen one had no right to have discovered so much about **love**, well, it couldn't be helped. It was the most thrilling, glorious, and beautiful thing in the world. It was like stained glass windows and sunsets and nightingales singing in the dark.
>
> —Frances Towers, *Tea with Mr. Rochester*, 1949

> For God's sake hold your tongue, and let me **love**,
>   Or chide my palsy, or my gout,
>   My five grey hairs, or ruined fortune flout,
> With wealth your state, your mind with arts improve,
>   Take you a course, get you a place,
>   Observe his Honour, or his Grace,
> Or the King's real, or his stamped face
>   Contemplate; what you will, approve,
>   So you will let me love.
>
> —John Donne, "The Canonization," 1633

[From Middle English, from Old English *lufu*; akin to German *Liebe* and Russian *lyubov'*, love, and Latin *libīdō*, desire.]

But one couldn't believe that reading *Jane Eyre* was wrong. And if it were, if at fourteen one had no right to have discovered so much about **love**, well, it couldn't be helped. It was the most thrilling, glorious, and beautiful thing in the world. It was like stained glass windows and sunsets and nightingales singing in the dark.

—Frances Towers, *Tea with Mr. Rochester*, 1949

59 **lurid** (lŏŏr′ĭd)

adjective

Characterized by shocking or outrageous behavior.

> There came a wild rush of anthropological lore into her brain, a flare of indecorous humor. It was one of the secret troubles of her mind, this grotesque twist her ideas would sometimes take, as though they rebelled and rioted. After all, she found herself reflecting, behind her aunt's complacent visage there was a past as **lurid** as anyone's—not, of course, her aunt's own personal past, which was apparently just that curate and almost incredibly jejune, but an ancestral past with all sorts of scandalous things in it: fire and slaughterings, exogamy, marriage by capture, corroborees, cannibalism! Ancestresses with perhaps dim anticipatory likenesses to her aunt, their hair less neatly done, no doubt, their manners and gestures as yet undisciplined, but still ancestresses in the direct line, must have danced through a brief and stirring life in the woady buff.
>
> —H. G. Wells, *Ann Veronica: A Modern Love Story*, 1909

[From Early Modern English *lurid*, pale, ghastly, from Latin *lūridus*, pale, from *lūror*, paleness.]

---

luscious (lŭsh′əs)

adjective

Having strong sensual or sexual appeal; seductive.

> We lay there awhile longer, but because I was a guest at the hotel and if anyone saw him coming out of my room it could ruin his chances of working here, he got up in the middle of the night, put his clothes on and gave me another of those **luscious** please-don't-go kisses and left quietly.
>
> —Terry McMillan, *How Stella Got Her Groove Back*, 1996

[From Middle English *lucius*, alteration of *licious*, perhaps short for *delicious*, delicious, from Late Latin *dēliciōsus*, pleasing, from Latin *dēlicia*, pleasure : *dē-*, intensive prefix + *lacere*, to entice.]

lustrous (lŭs′trəs)

adjective

Gleaming with brilliant light; radiant.

> The next moment, almost, one of the red roses of her crown broke loose from its fastenings and fell at his very feet. His countenance changed so that it seemed, for a second, to lose some of its color. He stooped and picked the rose up and held it in his hand. But Mistress Clorinda was looking at my Lord of Dunstanwolde, who was moving through the crowd to greet her. She gave him a brilliant smile, and from her **lustrous** eyes surely there passed something which lit a fire of hope in his.
>
> —Frances Hodgson Burnett, *A Lady of Quality*, 1896

> The little tuft of hair coming up over the crown, the **lustrous** eyes, the gorgeous shoulder line—and those sleeves I adore, regal, Florentine, diabolistic! I saw nothing below the bosom. I was too excited to stand off and survey you. How much I wanted to whisk you away—away forever. Eloping with the Infanta—ye gods.
>
> —Henry Miller, from a letter to Anaïs Nin, 1932

[Formed in Early Modern English from *lustre*, luster, from French, from Old French, from Old Italian *lustro*, from *lustrare*, to make bright, from Latin *lūstrāre*, from *lūstrum*, purification.]

osculation (ŏs′kyə-lā′shən)

noun

1. The act of kissing. **2.** A kiss.

> Then the bell rang, from the house. It was that same ring
> I had heard the week-end before, in the rhythm of my
> own name. Lily stood still, and listened. Wind-distorted,
> the bell rang again.
> "Nich-o-las." She looked mock-grave. "It tolls for thee."
> I looked up through the trees.
> "I can't think why."
> "You must go."
> "Will you come with me?" She shook her head. "Why
> not?"
> "Because it did not toll for me."
> "I think we ought to show that we're friends again."
> She was standing close to me, holding her hair from
> blowing across her face. She gave me a severe look.
> "Mr. Urfe!" She said it exactly as she had the night be-
> fore, the same chilly over-precise pronunciation. "Are
> you asking me to commit **osculation**?"
>
> —John Fowles, *The Magus: A Revised Version*,
> 1977

> Could it be that De Stancy was going to do what came
> next in the stage direction—kiss her? Before there was
> time for conjecture on that point, the sound of a very
> sweet and long-drawn **osculation** spread through the
> room, followed by loud applause from the people in the
> cheap seats.
>
> —Thomas Hardy, *A Laodicean*, 1881

[From Latin *ōsculātiō, ōsculātiōn-*, from *ōsculārī, ōsculāt-*,
from *ōsculum*, kiss, diminutive of *ōs*, mouth.]

palpitate (păl'pĭ-tāt')

verb

To beat with excessive rapidity; throb.

> Here I say I have amused myself in reading and thinking of my absent Friend, sometimes with a mixture of paine, sometimes with pleasure, sometimes anticipating a joyfull and happy meeting, whilst my Heart would bound and **palpitate** with the pleasing Idea, and with the purest affection I have held you to my Bosom till my whole Soul has dissolved in Tenderness and my pen fallen from my Hand.
>
> —Abigail Adams, from a letter to John Adams (in its original spelling), August 29, 1776

[From Latin *palpitāre*, *palpitāt-*, to move frequently and quickly, tremble, throb, from *palpāre*, to touch gently.]

passion (păsh'ən)

noun

A strong sexual desire or love for someone.

> Slowly and with great tenderness and delicacy Edwin helped Emma to overcome her terror, her reticence, and her inherent shyness. In spite of their mutual virginity, Edwin began to make love to Emma, and eventually she to him, under his softly whispered guidance. His desire flared into a **passion** he could no longer check, and it was this passion that imbued in him a finesse that was unconscious yet remarkable in its expertise.
>
> —Barbara Taylor Bradford, *A Woman of Substance*, 1979

After all Lytton, you are the only person who I have ever had an absorbing **passion** for. I shall never have another. I couldn't now—I had one of the most self-abasing loves that a person can have. You could throw me into transports of happiness and dash me into deluges of tears and despair, all by a few words. But these aren't reproaches. . . . Of course these years at Tidmarsh when we were quite alone will always be the happiest I ever spent. And I've such a store of good things which I've saved up, that I feel I could never be lonely again now. Still it's too much of a strain to be quite alone here waiting to see you or craning my nose and eyes out of the top window of 41 G. S. [Gordon Square] to see if you are coming down the street.

—Dora Carrington, from a letter to Lytton
Strachey, May 1921

[From Middle English, from Old French, from Medieval Latin *passiō*, *passiōn-*, sufferings of Jesus or a martyr, from Late Latin, physical suffering, martyrdom, sinful desire, from Latin, a suffering, an enduring, from *passus*, past participle of *patī*, to suffer.]

pine (pīn)

verb

To feel a lingering, often nostalgic desire.

How many weeping eyes I made to **pine** in woe;
How many sighing hearts I have not skill to show,
But I the prouder grew, and still this spake therefore:

"Go, go, go seek some otherwhere, importune me no
more."

—Queen Elizabeth I, "When I was Fair and Young,"
late 16th century

[From Middle English *pinen*, from Old English *pīnian*, to
cause to suffer, from *pīne, pain, from Vulgar Latin *pēna,
penalty, variant of Latin *poena*, from Greek *poinē*.]

66 pulchritude (pŭl′krĭ-to͞od′)

noun

Great physical beauty.

> **Pulchritude.** From the Latin, *pulcher*, beautiful. That was
> the word that first struck Joyce when Millat Iqbal stepped
> forward onto the steps of her conservatory, sneering at
> Marcus's bad jokes, shading his violet eyes from a fading
> winter sun. Pulchritude: not just the concept but the
> whole physical word appeared before her as if someone
> had typed it onto her retina—P u l c h r i t u d e—beauty
> where you would least suspect it, hidden in a word that
> looked like it should signify a belch or a skin infection.
> Beauty in a tall brown young man who should have been
> indistinguishable to Joyce from those she regularly
> bought milk and bread from, gave her accounts to for in-
> spection, or passed her checkbook to behind the thick
> glass of a bank till.
>
> —Zadie Smith, *White Teeth*, 2000

[From Middle English *pulcritude*, from Latin *pulchritūdō*,
from *pulcher*, beautiful.]

randy (răn′dē)

adjective

Feeling strong, especially uninhibited sexual desire.

> The Long Night's Moon breathed its light down on us, pale and faint. I placed my glass of chardonnay on the bench, feeling **randy** on account of my power struggles with the aforementioned novice-boy-librarian, who's about as sexy as he is colossally irritating.
>
> —Yxta Maya Murray, "The Lunalía," *Juicy Mangos*, 2007

[From Scottish English *randy*, rude, having a foul mouth, and dialectal British English *randy*, boisterous, unruly, possibly from obsolete English *rand*, to rant, from obsolete Dutch *randen*, *randten*, *ranten*, to rave, talk foolishly; akin to German *ranzen*, to spring about, be lascivious.]

rapturous (răp′chər-əs)

adjective

Filled with or characterized by great joy; ecstatic.

> And, even yet, I dare not let it languish,
>   Dare not indulge in memory's **rapturous** pain;
> Once drinking deep of that divinest anguish,
>   How could I seek the empty world again?
>
> —Emily Brontë, "Remembrance," 1846

[From *rapture* (from obsolete French, abduction, carrying off, from *rapt*, carried away, from Old French *rat*, from Latin *raptus*, past participle of *rapere*, to seize) + *-ous*, adjective suffix.]

ravish (răv′ĭsh)

verb

To overwhelm with emotion; enrapture.

> Do not threat me even in jest. I have been astonished that Men could die Martyrs for religion—I have shudder'd at it. I shudder no more—I could be martyr'd for my Religion—Love is my religion—I could die for that. I could die for you. My Creed is Love and you are its only tenet. You have **ravish'd** me away by a power I cannot resist; and yet I could resist till I saw you; and even since I have seen you I have endeavored often to "reason against the reasons of my love." I can do that no more—the pain would be too great. My love is selfish. I cannot breathe without you.
>
> Yours for ever
John Keats
>
> —John Keats, from a letter to Fanny Brawne (in its original spelling), October 13, 1819

[From Middle English *ravisshen*, from Old French *ravir*, *raviss-*, from Vulgar Latin **rapīre*, from Latin *rapere*, to seize.]

You have **ravish'd** me away by a power I cannot resist; and yet I could resist till I saw you; and even since I have seen you I have endeavored often to "reason against the reasons of my love." I can do that no more—the pain would be too great. My love is selfish. I cannot breathe without you.

—John Keats, from a letter to Fanny Brawne (in its original spelling), October 13, 1819

requite (rĭ-kwīt′)

verb

1. To pay someone back for something. **2.** To feel love in response to the love of someone else.

> BEATRICE: What fire is in mine ears? Can this be true?
> Stand I condemn'd for pride and scorn so much?
> Contempt, farewell, and maiden pride, adieu!
> No glory lives behind the back of such.
> And, Benedick, love on, I will **requite** thee,
> Taming my wild heart to thy loving hand.
> If thou dost love, my kindness shall incite thee
> To bind our loves up in a holy band;
> For others say thou dost deserve, and I
> Believe it better than reportingly.
>
> —William Shakespeare, *Much Ado About Nothing*,
> around 1598

[From Middle English *requiten* : *re-*, back (from Old French, from Latin) + *quiten*, to pay, repay (from Old French *quiter*, to release someone from a debt or obligation, from Medieval Latin *quiētāre*, *quītāre*, from Latin *quiētus*, at rest, past participle of *quiēscere*, to rest).]

romance (rō-măns′, rō′măns′)

noun

1. A sexual relationship; a love affair. **2.** Ardent emotional attachment or involvement between people; love.

verb

To court or woo.

> It amazed him—he had never been in such a beautiful house before. But what gave it an air of breathless intensity was that Daisy lived there—it was as casual a thing to her as his tent out at camp was to him. There was a ripe mystery about it, a hint of bedrooms upstairs more beautiful and cool than other bedrooms, of gay and radiant activities taking place through its corridors and of **romances** that were not musty and laid away already in lavender but fresh and breathing and redolent of this year's shining motor cars and of dances whose flowers were scarcely withered.
>
> —F. Scott Fitzgerald, *The Great Gatsby*, 1925

> EUNICE: As the years go by, **romance** fades and something else takes its place. Do you know what that is?
> HOWARD: Senility?
> EUNICE: *Trust*!
> HOWARD: That's what I meant.
>
> —from the film *What's Up, Doc?*, 1972

DR. MILES J. BENNELL: This is the oddest thing I've ever heard of. Let's hope we don't catch it. I'd hate to wake up some morning and find out that you weren't you.

BECKY DRISCOLL [*laughs*]: I'm not the high school kid you used to **romance**, so how can you tell?

DR. MILES J. BENNELL: You really want to know?

BECKY DRISCOLL: Mmm-hmm. [*They kiss.*]

DR. MILES J. BENNELL: Mmmm, you're Becky Driscoll.

—from the film *Invasion of the Body Snatchers*, 1956

[From Middle English, from Old French *romans*, *romance*, work written in French, from Vulgar Latin **rōmānicē* (*scrībere*), (to write) in the vernacular, from Latin *Rōmānicus*, Roman, from *Rōmānus*, Roman, from *Rōma*, Rome.]

seductive (sĭ-dŭk′tĭv)

adjective

Causing one to feel sexual desire; alluring.

Had kind fate but willed her to be born a gentlewoman of high degree in her own right and had she only received the benefit of a good education Gerty MacDowell might easily have held her own beside any lady in the land and have seen herself exquisitely gowned with jewels on her brow and patrician suitors at her feet vying with one another to pay their devoirs to her. Mayhap it was this, the love that might have been, that lent to her softlyfeatured face at whiles a look, tense with suppressed meaning, that imparted a strange yearning tendency to the beautiful eyes, a charm few could resist. Why have women such eyes of witchery? Gerty's were of the bluest Irish blue, set off by lustrous lashes and dark expressive brows. Time was when those brows were not so silkily **seductive**. It was Madame Vera Verity, directress of the Woman Beautiful page of the Princess novelette, who had first advised her to try eyebrowleine which gave that haunting expression to the eyes, so becoming in leaders of fashion, and she had never regretted it.

—James Joyce, *Ulysses* (in its original spelling), 1922

She regarded him with her kindly glances, which made something glow and expand within his chest. It was a delicious feeling, even though it did cut one's breath short now and then. Ecstatically he drank in the sound of her tranquil, **seductive** talk full of innocent gaiety and of spiritual quietude. His passion appeared to him to flame up and envelop her in blue fiery tongues from head to foot and over her head, while her soul reposed in the centre like a big white rose.

—Joseph Conrad, "The Warrior's Soul," 1917

[From Latin *sēdūcere*, *sēduct-*, to lead astray : *sē-*, apart + *dūcere*, to lead.]

sensual (sĕn′shoō-əl)

adjective

1. Relating to or providing gratification of the physical and especially the sexual appetites. **2.** Suggesting sexuality; voluptuous.

> It was a night of **sensual** passion, in which she was a little startled, and almost unwilling: yet pierced again with piercing thrills of sensuality, different, sharper, more terrible than the thrills of tenderness, but, at the moment, more desirable. Though a little frightened, she let him have his way, and the reckless, shameless sensuality shook her to her foundations, stripped her to the very last, and made a different woman of her. It was not really love. It was not voluptuousness. It was sensuality sharp and searing as fire, burning the soul to tinder.
>
> —D. H. Lawrence, *Lady Chatterley's Lover*, 1928

[From Middle English, from Late Latin *sēnsuālis*, from *sēnsus*, the faculty of perceiving, from *sentīre*, to feel.]

serenade (sĕr′ə-nād′, sĕr′ə-nād′)

noun

A musical performance given to express love for someone.

verb

To perform a serenade for someone.

> From me to thee glad **serenades**,
> Dances for thee I propose saluting thee, adornments
>   and feastings for thee,
> And the sights of the open landscape and the high-
>   spread sky are fitting,
> And life and the fields, and the huge and thoughtful
>   night.
>
> —Walt Whitman, "When Lilacs Last in the
>   Dooryard Bloom'd," 1855

> Marie pulled a dark purple silk necktie from her workbasket. "I knit this for him. It's a good color, don't you think? Will you please put it in with your things and tell him it's from me, to wear when he goes **serenading**."
>
> Alexandra laughed. "I don't believe he goes serenading much. He says in one letter that the Mexican ladies are said to be very beautiful, but that don't seem to me very warm praise."
>
> Marie tossed her head. "Emil can't fool me. If he's bought a guitar, he goes serenading. Who wouldn't, with all those Spanish girls dropping flowers down from their windows! I'd sing to them every night, wouldn't you, Mrs. Lee?"
>
> —Willa Cather, *O Pioneers!*, 1913

[From French *sérénade*, from Italian *serenata*, from *sereno*, calm, clear, the open air, from Latin *serēnus*.]

smitten (smĭt′n)

adjective

Affected sharply or deeply by sexual desire or love.

> At the captain's table one evening early in the voyage, she confessed to never having entertained the notion of going out to India, or of becoming the wife of an East India Company official. The prospects of marriage and of managing the house and domestic affairs of a high-ranking, socially demanding East India Company director turned her giddy. Thereafter, the captain was **smitten**.
>
> —Bharati Mukherjee, *The Tree Bride*, 2004

[Past participle of *to smite*, from Middle English *smiten*, to smite (perhaps originally, to slap mud on walls in wattle and daub construction), from Old English *smītan*, to daub, smear.]

soulmate (sōl′māt′)

noun

A person who is perfectly suited to another as a romantic partner.

> Over the summer, after years of being miserably single, Donna had met her **soulmate**—an overbearing optometrist named Bruce DeMastro—through an internet matchmaking service, and they'd gotten engaged after two magical dates.
>
> —Tom Perrotta, *The Abstinence Teacher*, 2007

[Formed in the 1800s from *soul* (from Middle English, from Old English *sāwol*; akin to German *Seele*) + *mate* (from Middle English, from Middle Low German *mat*, mate, originally meaning messmate, person one shares food with; akin to English *meat*, originally meaning food).]

spurn (spûrn)

verb

1. To reject someone disdainfully or contemptuously; scorn. **2.** To reject something contemptuously.

> Mina knew what Bradley should be doing every second of the day. He had **spurned** her, used her and spurned her, taken her virtue and discarded her like an old rag (Mina read a lot of cheap fiction), but Mina still loved him, her heart would always belong to him.
>
> —Kate Atkinson, *Human Croquet*, 1997

> What a triumph for him, as she often thought, could he know that the proposals which she had proudly **spurned** only four months ago, would now have been gladly and gratefully received! . . . She began now to comprehend that he was exactly the man, who, in disposition and talents, would most suit her.
>
> —Jane Austen, *Pride and Prejudice*, 1813

[From Middle English *spurnen*, to kick, spurn, from Old English *spurnan*; akin to Old English *spura*, spur.]

star-crossed (stär′krôst′)

adjective

Opposed by fate; ill-fated.

> Two households, both alike in dignity,
> In fair Verona, where we lay our scene,
> From ancient grudge break to new mutiny,
> Where civil blood makes civil hands unclean.
> From forth the fatal loins of these two foes
> A pair of **star-cross'd** lovers take their life;
> Whose misadventur'd piteous overthrows
> Doth with their death bury their parents' strife.
>
> —William Shakespeare, *Romeo and Juliet*, around 1595

[Literally, thwarted by the influence of an unlucky star : *star* (from Middle English *sterre*, from Old English *steorra*; akin to Greek *astēr* and Latin *stēlla*, star) + *crossed*, past participle of to cross (from Middle English *crossen*, to place crosswise, from *cros*, cross, from Old English, probably from Old Norse *kross*, from Old Irish *cros*, from Latin *crux*).]

succumb (sə-kŭm′)

verb

To submit to an overpowering force or yield to an overwhelming desire; give up or give in.

> The very next day she arrived in the back alleyway at exactly the same time and, catching sight of Hungry Hop again—for it was his regularly assigned bath hour—she threw him a rose. This time, Hungry Hop, his heart aflutter, **succumbed** to the mysterious compulsion welling up inside him and responded with his mother's hairnet. This incident marked an important change in their relationship: the beginning of a mutual involvement, a series of feverish exchanges that took place almost daily, with Pinky hovering about his house with some token of affection in her pocket and Hungry Hop waiting by the bathroom window. As the days went by, they managed to exchange all manner of bottles, toffees, sweetmeats, handkerchiefs and nightclothes.
>
> —Kiran Desai, *Hullabaloo in the Guava Orchard*, 1999

> He kissed her. There was such an incredible logic to kissing, such a metal-to-magnet pull between two people that it was a wonder that they found the strength to prevent themselves from **succumbing** every second. Rightfully, the world should be a whirlpool of kissing into which we sank and never found the strength to rise up again.
>
> —Ann Patchett, *Bel Canto*, 2001

[From Middle English *succomben*, to bring down, from Old French *succomber*, from Latin *succumbere*, to lie under, yield : *sub-*, under + *-cumbere*, to lie down (as in *accumbere*, to lie down).]

He kissed her. There was such an incredible logic to kissing, such a metal-to-magnet pull between two people that it was a wonder that they found the strength to prevent themselves from **succumbing** every second. Rightfully, the world should be a whirlpool of kissing into which we sank and never found the strength to rise up again.

—Ann Patchett, *Bel Canto*, 2001

sultry (sŭl′trē)

adjective

Expressing or arousing sexual desire.

> Eat thou and drink; to-morrow thou shalt die.
>> Surely the earth, that's wise being very old,
>> Needs not our help. Then loose me, love, and hold
> Thy **sultry** hair up from my face; that I
> May pour for thee this golden wine, brim-high,
>> Till round the glass thy fingers glow like gold.
>> We'll drown all hours: thy song, while hours are tolled,
> Shall leap, as fountains veil the changing sky.

—Dante Gabriel Rossetti, "The House of Life,"
1881

The city was always better than anywhere else for filming, Castle and all. Go to Rumania and you'd find the castles still full of manacled prisoners clanking their chains; try Poland and you'd have to fly in special food for your stars; in Hungary the cameraman would have artistic tantrums; but here in the city there would be gaiety, fun, sometimes even sparkle, the clatter of high heels on cobblestones, **sultry** looks from sultry eyes, and of course nights with Milena in the fringy, shabby apartment, with the high, white-mantled brass bed.

—Fay Weldon "Wasted Lives," *Wicked Women*,
1972

[From obsolete *sulter*, to swelter, possibly alteration of *swelter*, from Middle English *swelteren*, to be faint from heat, from *swelten*, to die.]

---

sweetheart (swēt′härt′)

noun

1. A person who is loved by someone else, especially in a sexual relationship. **2.** Used as a familiar term of endearment for such a person.

> **Sweetheart**, do not love too long:
> I loved long and long,
> And grew to be out of fashion
> Like an old song.
>
> All through the years of our youth
> Neither could have known
> Their own thought from the other's,
> We were so much at one.
>
> But O, in a minute she changed—
> O do not love too long,
> Or you will grow out of fashion
> Like an old song.
>
> —William Butler Yeats, "O Do Not Love Too Long,"
> 1904

[From Middle English *swete hert* : *swete*, sweet (from Old English *swēte*; akin to Latin *suāvis* and Greek *hēdus*, pleasant) + *hert*, heart (from Old English *heorte*; akin to Greek *kardiā*, heart).]

82 **swoon** (swoon)

verb

To be overwhelmed by ecstatic joy.

noun

A state of ecstasy or rapture.

> 'You boys are sentimental. Death *and* glory. A guy I know fell in love with me because of my laugh. We hadn't even met or been in the same room, he'd heard me on a tape.'
>   'And?'
>   'Oh, he **swooned** over me like a married man, made me fall in love with him. You've heard the story. How smart women become idiots, ignore everything they should keep on knowing. By the end I wasn't laughing too much. No bell-ringing.'
>
> —Michael Ondaatje, *Anil's Ghost: A Novel*, 2000

So, under the bridge, they came to a standstill, and he lifted her upon his breast. His body vibrated taut and powerful as he closed upon her and crushed her, breathless and dazed and destroyed, crushed her upon his breast. Ah, it was terrible, and perfect. Under this bridge, the colliers pressed their lovers to their breast. And now, under the bridge, the master of them all pressed her to himself! And how much more powerful and terrible was his embrace, than theirs, how much more concentrated and supreme his love was, than theirs, in the same sort! She felt she would **swoon**, die, under the vibrating, inhuman tension of his arms and his body—she would pass away. Then the unthinkable, high vibration slackened and became more undulating, he slackened and drew her with him to stand with his back to the wall.

> —D. H. Lawrence, *Women in Love*, 1920

How changed I found him, even in those few days! He lay an image of sadness and resignation waiting his death. Very young he looked; though his actual age was thirty-nine, one would have called him ten years younger, at least. He thought of Catherine; for he murmured her name. I touched his hand, and spoke.

"Catherine is coming, dear master!" I whispered; "she is alive and well; and will be here, I hope, to-night."

I trembled at the first effects of this intelligence: he half rose up, looked eagerly round the apartment, and then sank back in a **swoon**.

—Emily Brontë, *Wuthering Heights*, 1847

[From Middle English *swounen*, probably from *iswowen*, in a swoon, from Old English *geswōgen*, apparently a past participle of *swōgan*, to suffocate, as in *āswōgan*, to rush into, choke.]

83 **sympathy** (sĭm′pə-thē)

noun

Mutual understanding or affection between people, arising from a sense of identifying with another's feelings.

> They talked now as a doomed brother and sister might, renewing in each other the sense of relief which comes to those who find someone to share the burden of unconfessed preoccupations. In all this **sympathy** an unexpected shadow of desire stirred within them, a wraith merely, the stepchild of confession and release. . . . Loving is so much truer when sympathy and not desire makes the match; for it leaves no wounds.
>
> —Lawrence Durrell, *Justine*, 1957

> My ardent sensibilities incite me to love—to seek to inspire **sympathy**—to be beloved! My heart obstinately refuses to renounce the man, to whose mind my own seems akin! From the centre of private affections, it will at length embrace—like spreading circles on the peaceful bosom of the smooth and expanded lake—the whole sensitive and rational creation. Is it virtue, then, to combat, or to yield to, my passions?
>
> —Mary Hays, *Memoirs of Emma Courtney*, 1796

[From Latin *sympathīa*, from Greek *sumpatheia*, from *sumpathēs*, affected by like feelings : *sun-*, with + *pathos*, emotion.]

84 tenderness (tĕn′dər-nĕs)

noun

A state of feeling protective concern or sensitiveness for another.

> Last night, there was a moment before you got into bed. You stood, quite naked, bending forward a little—talking. It was only for an instant. I saw you—I loved you so—loved your body with such **tenderness**—Ah my dear—And I am not thinking of 'passion'. No, of that other thing that makes me feel that every inch of you is so precious to me. Your soft shoulders—your creamy warm skin, your ears, cold like shells are cold—your long legs and your feet that I love to clasp with my feet— the feeling of your belly—& your thin young back. . . . It is partly because we are young that I feel this tenderness.
>
> —Katherine Mansfield, from a letter to John Middleton Murry, May 19, 1917

[From Middle English, from *tender*, tender, from Old French *tendre*, from Latin *tener*.]

throb (thrŏb)

verb

To beat or pulsate rapidly or painfully.

> She turned now and started kissing me with such a hungry agony that my burnt shoulders began to **throb** until tears came into my eyes. "Ah!" she said softly and sadly. "You are crying. I wish I could. I have lost the knack."
>
> —Lawrence Durrell, *Justine*, 1957

> She was still half a mile from her destination, and she decided to walk across to Madison Avenue and take the electric car. As she turned into the side street, a vague memory stirred in her. The row of budding trees, the new brick and limestone house-fronts, the Georgian flathouse with flowerboxes on its balconies, were merged together into the setting of a familiar scene. It was down this street that she had walked with Selden, that September day two years ago; a few yards ahead was the doorway they had entered together. The recollection loosened a throng of benumbed sensations—longings, regrets, imaginings, the **throbbing** brood of the only spring her heart had ever known.
>
> —Edith Wharton, *The House of Mirth*, 1905

[From Middle English *throbben*, of onomatopoeic origin.]

---

throb / titillate

titillate (tĭt′l-āt′)

verb

To excite someone pleasurably or erotically.

> Delilah tried not to catch the meaning of that wink, although she felt an unexpected, and highly unwelcome, fluttering between her legs. What was the matter with her? Was she actually **titillated** by the vague boasting of this steroid-bound cretin?
>
> —Joy Fielding, *Heartstopper*, 2007

> His slow, green eyes **titillated** her, and from the first, he treated her with an air of grave, protective, exaggerated courtesy that charmed and soothed her.
>
> —Anne Rivers Siddons, *Heartbreak Hotel*, 1976

[From Latin *tītillāre*, *tītillāt-*, to tickle, of imitative origin, intended by its sound to suggest the action or sensation of tickling.]

torch (tôrch)

noun

Carry a torch: To have longstanding romantic feelings for someone, especially someone who does not feel or requite the feeling.

> "Well, she was his grand passion, that I know for a fact—because he once told me so. I believe he's **carrying a torch** for her."
>
> "That's a bit farfetched, Emily. They've been divorced for donkey's years."
>
> "Even so, he could have remained shackled to her emotionally." Emily tilted her blond head to one side and wrinkled her nose. "Unrequited love and all that. Why are you looking so skeptical, Grandma? Don't you believe that's possible?"
>
> —Barbara Taylor Bradford, *Hold the Dream*, 1985

[From Middle English *torche*, torch (as made by twisting around the end of a stick), from Old French, from Vulgar Latin **torca*, alteration of Latin *torqua*, variant of *torquēs*, twisted neck chain, wreath, from Latin *torquēre*, to twist.]

torrid (tôr′ĭd)

adjective

1. Parched with the heat of the sun; intensely hot. **2.** Passionate; ardent: *a torrid love scene.*

> Give me more love or more disdain;
>> The **torrid**, or the frozen zone,
> Bring equal ease unto my pain;
>> The temperate affords me none;
> Either extreme, of love, or hate,
> Is sweeter than a calm estate.
>
>> —Thomas Carew, "Mediocrity in Love Rejected," 1640

> MAX'S FATHER: All anybody wants to talk about today is the market. Such a bore! How's your sentimental life?
> MAX: **Torrid**. Yours?
> MAX'S FATHER: Arid—but sunny.
>
>> —from the film *Max*, 2002

[From Latin *torridus*, from *torrēre*, to parch; akin to English *thirst*.]

transfigure (trăns-fĭg′yər)

verb

To alter the appearance or nature of something, especially to a more exalted state; transform.

> But Lucy had developed since the spring. That is to say, she was now better able to stifle the emotions of which the conventions and the world disapprove. Though the danger was greater, she was not shaken by deep sobs. She said to Cecil, "I am not coming in to tea—tell mother—I must write some letters," and went up to her room. Then she prepared for action. Love felt and returned, love which our bodies exact and our hearts have **transfigured**, love which is the most real thing that we shall ever meet, reappeared now as the world's enemy, and she must stifle it.
>
> —E. M. Forster, *A Room With a View*, 1908

[From Middle English *transfiguren*, from Old French *transfigurer*, from Latin *trānsfigūrāre* : *trāns-*, across, beyond + *figūra*, form.]

transport (trăns′pôrt′)

verb

To move to strong emotion; carry away; enrapture.

noun

The condition of being moved deeply or passionately by desire or love.

> Anna did not receive the boy's letter in the Tyrol. It followed her to Oxford. She was just going out when it came, and she took it up with the mingled beatitude and almost sickening tremor that a lover feels touching the loved one's letter. She would not open it in the street, but carried it all the way to the garden of a certain College, and sat down to read it under the cedar-tree. That little letter, so short, boyish, and dry, **transported** her halfway to heaven.
>
> —John Galsworthy, *The Dark Flower*, 1913

Jesus! from whence and whither am I fallen? From the hopes of blissful exstasies to black despair! From the expectation of immortal **transports**, which none but your dear self can give me, and which none but he who loves like me could ever so much as think of, to a complication of cruel passions and the most dreadful condition of human life.

My fault indeed has been very great, and cries aloud for the severest vengeance. See it inflicted on me: see me despair and die for that fault. But let me not die unpardon'd, madam; I die for you, but die in the most cruel and dreadful manner. The wretch that lies broken on the wheel alive feels not a quarter of what I endure. Yet boundless love has been all my crime; unjust, ungrateful, barbarous return for it!

Suffer me to take my eternal leave of you; when I have done that how easy will it be to bid all the rest of the world adieu.

—William Congreve, from a letter to Arabella Hunt (in its original spelling), around 1700

He began by making many complaints of my unwillingness to trust myself with him, and begged to know what could be the reason. This question so much embarrassed me, that I could not tell what to answer, but only said, that I was sorry to have taken up so much of his time.

'O Miss Anville,' (cried he, taking my hand) 'if you knew with what **transport** I would dedicate to you not only the present but all the future time allotted to me, you would not injure me by making such an apology.'

—Frances Burney, *Evelina*, 1778

[From Middle English *transporten*, to convey, transfer, from Old French *transporter*, from Latin *trānsportāre* : *trāns-*, across + *portāre*, to carry.]

Anna did not receive the boy's letter in the Tyrol. It followed her to Oxford. She was just going out when it came, and she took it up with the mingled beatitude and almost sickening tremor that a lover feels touching the loved one's letter. She would not open it in the street, but carried it all the way to the garden of a certain College, and sat down to read it under the cedar-tree. That little letter, so short, boyish, and dry, **transported** her halfway to heaven.

—John Galsworthy, *The Dark Flower*, 1913

91

trifle (trī′fəl)

verb

To flirt with someone or cause someone to feel love when one is not serious.

> "Listen to me, Gladys. You and I understand each other only too well. We are two tired worldlings. There isn't really much that we could give each other."
>
> "You mean you've been **trifling** with me? Trifling with an innocent girl's affections?"
>
> "We could perhaps amuse each other for a season. We could even fancy that we were hurt, bereft . . ."
>
> "You won't marry me! Say it! You wouldn't have dared to treat me so had my old father lived! But I see it all. We are only the playthings of you men."
>
> "Gladys, if you will only be serious . . ."
>
> "Don't flatter yourself that nothing can make up for your withdrawn love. A diamond necklace might make all the difference."
>
> "What would Heyward say?"
>
> "I'd tell him it was paste. Haven't you read any French novels?"
>
> —Louis Auchincloss, *The House of the Prophet*, 1980

"If you *will* thank me," he replied, "let it be for yourself alone. That the wish of giving happiness to you, might add force to the other inducements which led me on, I

---

shall not attempt to deny. But your *family* owe me nothing. Much as I respect them, I believe, I thought only of *you*."

Elizabeth was too much embarrassed to say a word. After a short pause, her companion added, "You are too generous to **trifle** with me. If your feelings are still what they were last April, tell me so at once. *My* affections and wishes are unchanged, but one word from you will silence me on this subject for ever."

—Jane Austen, *Pride and Prejudice*, 1813

[From Middle English *trifle*, *trufle*, piece of nonsense, lie, joke, from Old French *trufle*, mockery, deception, from *truffe*, deception, probably from Provençal *trufa*, truffle (since truffles are difficult to discover).]

troth (trôth, trŏth, trōth)

noun

A promise to marry someone; a betrothal.

> He had not only promised falsely, but had made such promises with a deliberate, premeditated falsehood. And he had been selfish, coldly selfish, weighing the value of his own low lusts against that of her holy love. She had known this, and had parted from him with an oath to herself that no promised contrition on his part should ever bring them again together. But she had pardoned him as a man, though never as a lover, and had bade him welcome again as a cousin and as her friend's brother. She had again become very anxious as to his career, not hiding her regard, but professing that anxiety aloud. She knew him to be clever, ambitious, bold—and she believed even yet, in spite of her own experience, that he might not be bad at heart. Now, as she told herself that in truth she loved the man to whom her **troth** was plighted, I fear that she almost thought more of that other man from whom she had torn herself asunder.

—Anthony Trollope, *Can You Forgive Her?*, 1865

[From Middle English *trouthe*, *trothe*, honesty, a promise, *troth*, variant of *treuthe*, from Old English *trēowth*, truth.]

tryst (trĭst)

noun

1. An agreement between lovers to meet at a certain time and place in order to make love. **2.** A usually secret meeting between lovers for a sexual encounter.

verb

To keep a tryst.

> A: How do people marry, Mother?
> B: They strike a bargain.
> A: What's to bargain over if you're in love?
> B: Marriage is a contract, not a perpetual **tryst**.
> —from the film *Dangerous Beauty*, 1998

> FRASIER: Hello, Eileen, I'm listening.
> EILEEN: Dr. Crane, I've been very happily married for twenty years and I wouldn't dream of cheating, but lately when we're making love I find myself fantasizing about people . . . other than my husband.
> FRASIER: Well, that's perfectly normal. It's quite all right to spice up one's love life by imagining a **tryst** with, oh, a sports figure or a movie star or . . .
> EILEEN: Or a radio psychiatrist?
> —from the television show *Frasier*, 1995

[From Middle English *trist*, a place that hunters have designated for waiting for game, appointment, from Old French *triste*.]

94 **voluptuous** (və-lŭp′chŏŏ-əs)

adjective

Giving or characterized by strong sensual pleasure.

> The amenity of its climate, where the ardent heats of a southern summer were tempered by breezes from snow-clad mountains; the **voluptuous** repose of its valleys and the bosky luxuriance of its groves and gardens all awakened sensations of delight, and disposed the mind to love and poetry. Hence the great number of amatory poets that flourished in Granada.
>
> —Washington Irving, *The Alhambra*, 1832

> "Robert," she [Edna] said, "are you asleep?"
>
> "No," he answered, looking up at her.
>
> She leaned over and kissed him—a soft, cool, delicate kiss, whose **voluptuous** sting penetrated his whole being—then she moved away from him. He followed, and took her in his arms, just holding her close to him. She put her hand up to his face and pressed his cheek against her own. The action was full of love and tenderness. He sought her lips again. Then he drew her down upon the sofa beside him and held her hand in both of his.
>
> —Kate Chopin, *The Awakening*, 1899

[From Middle English, from Old French *voluptueux*, from Latin *voluptuōsus*, full of pleasure, from *voluptās*, pleasure.]

vow (vou)

noun

An earnest promise to perform a specified act or behave in a certain manner.

verb

To promise something solemnly; pledge.

> Roland had weakened her. With those lips of his brushing across hers, teasing her about all the lusciousness that could come, and with his hardened body rubbing hers, stirring her desire so powerfully, she had almost forgot her **vow**—her vow to seek a man who was the opposite of the ones who broke her mother's heart.
>
> —Louré Bussey, *A Taste of Love*, 1999

> I might have broken out into false swearing: **vowed** that I did love her; but I could not lie in her pure face: I could not perjure myself in her truthful presence. Besides, such hollow oaths would have been vain as void: she would no more have believed me than she would have believed the ghost of Judas, had he broken from the night and stood before her. Her female heart had finer perceptions than to be cheated into mistaking my half-coarse, half-cold admiration, for true-throbbing, manly love.
>
> —Charlotte Brontë, *Shirley*, 1849

[From Middle English *vou*, from Old French, from Latin *vō-tum*, from neuter past participle of *vovēre*, to vow.]

wanton (wŏn′tən)

adjective

Given to sexual extravagance; lascivious or lewd.

noun

One that is playful or frolicsome.

> Oh, think not I am faithful to a vow!
>   Faithless am I save to love's self alone.
>   Were you not lovely I would leave you now:
>   After the feet of beauty fly my own.
>   Were you not still my hunger's rarest food,
>   And water ever to my wildest thirst,
>   I would desert you—think not but I would!—
>   And seek another as I sought you first.
>   But you are mobile as the veering air,
>   And all your charms more changeful than the tide,
>   Wherefore to be inconstant is no care:
>   I have but to continue at your side.
>   So **wanton**, light and false, my love, are you,
>   I am most faithless when I most am true.
>
> > —Edna St. Vincent Millay, "Oh, think not I am
> > faithful to a vow!" 1920

Rob: Do you know how fine you are to me, Mary MacGregor? So fine.

Mary: Is that why you sent them away? To tell me how fine I am? Or did you want to make a silk purse out of my sow's ear again?

Rob: Tsk, tsk, tsk. What a **wanton** I'm wed to.

Mary: You know what the old wives say about these standing stones?

Rob: No. What do the old wives say . . . old wife?

Mary: They say the stones make men hard and women fertile.

Rob: We've no need of them, you and me.

Mary: You know how fine you are to me, Robert MacGregor?

—from the film *Rob Roy*, 1995

[From Middle English *wantowen*, undisciplined, lewd :
wan-, not, lacking (from Old English; akin to Modern
English *want*, from Old Norse *vanta*, to lack) + *towen*, past
participle of *teen*, to bring up, educate (from Old English
tēon, to lead, draw; akin to German *ziehen*).]

win (wĭn)

verb

To succeed in gaining the affection or love of someone, especially after a concerted effort.

> Why so pale and wan, fond lover?
>> Prithee, why so pale?
> Will, when looking well can't move her,
>> Looking ill prevail?
>> Prithee, why so pale?
>
> Why so dull and mute, young sinner?
>> Prithee, why so mute?
> Will, when speaking well can't **win** her,
>> Saying nothing do't?
>> Prithee, why so mute?
>
> Quit, quit for shame, this will not move,
>> This cannot take her;
> If of herself she will not love,
>> Nothing can make her;
>> The devil take her!
>
> —Sir John Suckling, "Song," 1638

He called on John Ferrier that night, and many times again, until his face was a familiar one at the farmhouse. John, cooped up in the valley, and absorbed in his work, had had little chance of learning the news of the outside world during the last twelve years. All this Jefferson Hope was able to tell him, and in a style which interested Lucy as well as her father. He had been a pioneer in California, and could narrate many a strange tale of fortunes made and fortunes lost in those wild, halcyon days. He had been a scout too, and a trapper, a silver explorer, and a ranchman. Wherever stirring adventures were to be had, Jefferson Hope had been there in search of them. He soon became a favourite with the old farmer, who spoke eloquently of his virtues. On such occasions, Lucy was silent, but her blushing cheek and her bright, happy eyes, showed only too clearly that her young heart was no longer her own. Her honest father may not have observed these symptoms, but they were assuredly not thrown away upon the man who had **won** her affections.

—Sir Arthur Conan Doyle, "A Study in Scarlet," 1887

[From Middle English *winnen*, from Old English *winnan*, to fight, strive; akin to German *gewinnen*, to gain, win.]

98 **WOO** (wo͞o)

verb

To try to gain the affection of someone with the intent of entering a sexual relationship.

> "I believe a person could fix anything," she says in the house utensils aisle, "given proper instruction and duct tape." Then she adds, "Except trust." And this is the first hint she's given of what keeps her so clearly focused on staying "neighborly."
>
> Not that he's done much more than buddy his grocery cart up to hers, and although it's true, the contents have more and more begun to resemble hers, still he keeps a cautious distance. He's at a standstill, and all the month of long hours mulling over the mop handle at work, dreaming up ways to **woo** and win her, have yielded nothing more than any neighbor could claim.
>
> Until today, when she lets slip the tidbit about trust.
>
> —Claire Davis "Labors of the Heart," 2000

KATHARINE [HEPBURN]: Heard you were **wooing** Ginger Rogers. What about that?

HOWARD [HUGHES]: She's just a friend.

KATHARINE: Ha! Men can't be friends with women, Howard. They must possess them or leave them be. It's a primitive urge from caveman days. It's all in Darwin. Hunt the flesh, kill the flesh, eat the flesh. That's the male sex all over.

HOWARD: Excuse me?

KATHARINE: Well, if you're deaf, you must own up to it. Get a hearing aid. Or see my father. He's a urologist, but it's all tied up inside the body, don't you find? Me, I keep healthy. I take seven showers a day to keep clean. Also because I am what's so vulgarly referred to as "out-

---

doorsy." Well, I'm not outdoorsy. I'm athletic. I sweat. There it is. Now we both know the sordid truth. I sweat and you're deaf. Aren't we a fine pair of misfits?

[*She putts her golf ball into the hole.*]

Three.

[*Howard putts his ball just short of the hole. She knocks it in with her club.*]

Noble effort.

[*She retrieves his ball from the hole and tosses it to him.*]

So I suppose you're wooing me now?

—from the film *The Aviator*, 2004

[From Middle English *wowen*, from Old English *wōgian*.]

99 yearn (yûrn)

verb

To have a strong, often sad or painful romantic desire.

> O flames that glowed! O hearts that **yearned**!
>   They were indeed too much akin,
> The drift-wood fire without that burned,
>   The thoughts that burned and glowed within.
>
> —Henry Wadsworth Longfellow, "The Fire of Drift-Wood," around 1850

> From the moonlight and streetlight coming in through the window, I saw his body beautifully sculpted by light and shadows. I did yearn for him, but I **yearned** for so much more along with that body, which I must have sensed Rudy would never give me. He was worn down with frustration, he said. I was cruel. I didn't understand that unlike a girl, it was physically painful for guys not to have sex. He thought it was time to call it quits. I was tearful and pleading: I wanted to feel we were serious about each other before we made love. "Serious!" He made a face. "How about fun? Fun, you know?"
>
> —Julia Alvarez, *How the García Girls Lost Their Accents*, 1991

[From Middle English *yernen*, from Old English *geornan*, *giernan*; akin to German *begehren*, to desire.]

zaftig (zäf′tĭk, zäf′tĭg)

adjective

Having a full, shapely figure.

> Mrs. Zender swept her arm in the direction of the back of the house. The hallway was wide enough to allow them to walk side by side, but Mrs. Zender walked ahead. She was tall, and she was **zaftig**. Definitely zaftig. She was also majestic. She moved forward like a queen vessel plowing still waters. Her kimono corrugated as she moved. There was a thin stripe of purple that winked as it appeared and then disappeared in a fold of fabric at her waist.
>
> —E. L. Konigsburg, *The Mysterious Edge of the Heroic World*, 2007

[From Yiddish *zaftik*, juicy, from Middle High German *saftec*, from *saft*, juice, from Old High German *saf*; akin to English *sap*.]

The 100 Words

adore
affair
affection
alluring
amorous
ardor
assignation
attentions
beloved
besotted
bewitching
billet-doux
bliss
blush
buss
callipygian
canoodle
caress
charm
chaste
clandestine
comely
companionship
conjugal
constant
coy
crush
cute
dalliance
desire
dishabille
ecstasy
embrace
enamor

enchant
entrance
entreaty
erotic
escort
flame
fling
flirt
fluster
gallant
heartthrob
idolize
illicit
inamorata
infatuation
inflame
intimate
intoxicating
jealousy
jilt
kiss
languor
liaison
love
lurid
luscious
lustrous
osculation
palpitate
passion
pine
pulchritude
randy
rapturous

ravish
requite
romance
seductive
sensual
serenade
smitten
soulmate
spurn
star-crossed
succumb
sultry
sweetheart
swoon
sympathy
tenderness
throb
titillate
torch
torrid
transfigure
transport
trifle
troth
tryst
voluptuous
vow
wanton
win
woo
yearn
zaftig